'...er despair lightly and artfully, with ...ch gentle good nature that we forgot how sad she ... Seeing Long's capacity for wonder and even contentment in ...ist of her sadness feels like seeing tiny shoots of grass peeking from ...ash in a landscape stripped bare by fire. Her memoir ... intersperses the ...ory of her mushroom education with details of her emotional journey, ...h informing the other. She is a fine anthropologist of both ... At its ...ntre, this book poses a familiar, awful existential question. How do you ...on living when the person you loved so much — perhaps the person you ...ved best in the world — is gone?' **Sarah Lyall, *The New York Times***

'...ong's book, in which she recounts how mycology helped her to recover ...om the death of her husband, could hardly be better timed ... People ...lk, in these fractious times, about mindfulness. They wonder how to ...ut out the din, and get back to the important, elemental things in life. ...lushrooms, here only fleetingly and easily damaged, do this effortlessly.' **...achel Cooke, *The Observer***

'...her search for new meaning in life after the death of her husband, Long ...tt Woon undertook the study of mushrooms. What she found in the ...ods, and expresses with such tender joy in this heartfelt memoir, was ...thing less than salvation.' **Eugenia Bone, author of *Mycophilia***

'...this enchanting debut memoir, anthropologist Long tells of her life in Norway after the sudden death of her 54-year-old husband left her "alone ...the world". A beginner's course in mushrooming was an unexpected ...aft, leading her to find community and a sense of meaning while ...ndering the woods ... This unique tale of rebirth after loss doubles as a riveting foray into the world of mushrooming.' ***Publishers Weekly***

'*The Way Through the Woods* was enchanting, made me want to go mushroom picking and learn how to do it properly!' **Megha Majumdar, author of A Burning**

'It is poetic, warm and moving, and steeped in life wisdom.' **Sissel Gran, Norwegian psychologist and author**

'A book that's emotional and elegant, and above all, scientific.' **Francesca Frediani, *La Repubblica***

'An ode to resilience, humour and change.' ***Simple Things***

'A universe that seems made of equal parts Elsa Beskow and the Grimm brothers ... Long Litt Woon's attention to the smallest details in grief and mourning makes the book breath-taking to read.' **Karen Syberg, Danish author**

'Anyone with an interest in the natural world will delight in Long's sharp-eyed descriptions (and line drawings) of fungi and her therapeutic rambles through Norwegian woods. A wonder-inducing dive into the unique kingdom of fungi.' ***Kirkus***

'Enchanting, original, and moving.' **The Nan Shepherd Prize (Book of the Week)**

'Like mushrooms themselves, *The Way Through the Woods* is surprising, comforting, and completely engrossing. Woon takes us foraging not just through the fascinating world of fungi but also through her personal grief. Like *The Sound of a Wild Snail Eating* and *H is for Hawk* her gorgeous, intimate encounter with unfamiliar species teaches us that observing nature carefully is both inspiring and healing.' **Juli Berwald, author of *Spineless: the science of jellyfish and the art of growing a backbone***

'Among the 20 "utterly engrossing" non-fiction books for the summer of 2019.' ***Bookbub***

'*The Way Through the Woods* will make a lovely gift for the curious bushwalker, recently bereaved person, or even the niche hobbyist in your life.' **Georgia Delaney, *Readings***

'A heartfelt and honest account of overcoming loss that will give hope to readers in a simple, yet profound way. In her beautifully written first book, Long shares a way to feel anew by setting foot on a different path, discovering a spark of joy, and finding meaning again. Readers who appreciate the journeys through grief found in memoirs like Cheryl Strayed's *Wild* (2012) or Shannon Leone Fowler's *Travelling with Ghosts* (2017) should pick this up.' **Melissa Norstedt, *Booklist***

'This thoughtful, touching account explores Woon's experience learning mushroom foraging in the aftermath of tragedy ... With charming sketches of the various mushrooms Woon encounters, this moving memoir explores one woman's journey through grief and will please fans of personal narrative as well as those who may be interested in mushroom foraging.' **Vanessa Hughes, *Library Journal***

'Existential questions as tasty as morels.' ***L'Obs***

LONGLISTED FOR THE JAN MICHALSKI PRIZE FOR LITERATURE 2019

The way through the woods

LONG LITT WOON (born 1958 in Malaysia)
is an anthropologist and Norwegian Mycological
Association-certified mushroom professional. She
first visited Norway as a young exchange student.
There she met and married Norwegian Eiolf Olsen.
She currently lives in Oslo, Norway. According to
Chinese naming tradition, 'Long' is her surname
and 'Litt Woon' her first name.

BARBARA J. HAVELAND (born 1951) is a Scots-
born literary translator resident in Copenhagen.
She translates fiction, poetry, and drama from
Norwegian and Danish to English, and has
translated works by many leading Danish and
Norwegian writers. Her most recent published
works include new translations of *The Master Builder*
and *Little Eyolf* by Henrik Ibsen and the first two
volumes of Carl Frode Tiller's *Encircling* trilogy.

THE
WAY
THROUGH
THE
WOODS

OVERCOMING GRIEF THROUGH NATURE

LONG LITT WOON

SCRIBE

Melbourne • London

Scribe Publications
2 John St, Clerkenwell, London, WC1N 2ES, United Kingdom
18–20 Edward St, Brunswick, Victoria 3056, Australia

Originally published in Norwegian as *Stien tilbake til livet. Om sopp og sorg*
by Vigmostad & Bjørke 2017
First published in English by Scribe 2019
This edition published 2021

Text copyright © Long Litt Woon 2017
Translation copyright © Barbara J. Haveland 2019
Illustrations copyright © Oona Viskari 2018, 2019

All rights reserved. Without limiting the rights under copyright reserved above,
no part of this publication may be reproduced, stored in or introduced into a retrieval system,
or transmitted, in any form or by any means (electronic, mechanical, photocopying, recording
or otherwise) without the prior written permission of the publishers of this book.

Every effort has been made to ensure the accuracy of the information in this book. However,
neither the author nor the publisher shall be liable or responsible for any loss or damage
allegedly arising from any information or suggestion in this book.

Extract from the poem 'Another Sun' on p. xi from the poetry collection *En annen sol* by Kolbein
Falkeid © Cappelen Damm AS 1989. Reproduced with permission.
Table of mushroom smells on p. 168 from *Svampe* Issue 9 (1984). Reproduced with permission.
List of psilocybin trip levels on pp. 216–17 quoted from www.shroomery.org. Reproduced with
permission.

The moral rights of the author and translator have been asserted.

Typeset in Portrait and Brandon by the publisher
Printed and bound in the UK by CPI Group (UK) Ltd, Croydon CR0 4YY

Scribe Publications is committed to the sustainable use of natural resources
and the use of paper products made responsibly from those resources.

9781911617389 (UK edition)
9781925713213 (Australian edition)
9781925693850 (ebook)

This translation has been published with the financial support of NORLA.

Catalogue records for this book are available from the National Library of Australia and the
British Library.

scribepublications.co.uk
scribepublications.com.au

Memoria In Aeterna,
Eiolf Olsen (1955–2010)

Still round the boat, still
as stars when the earth is unscrewed and mankind's words,
fumbling thoughts and dreams forgotten.
I place the oars, each in its rowlock,
dip and raise them. Listen.
The little splash of drops in the ocean
cements the stillness. Slowly, towards another sun,
I turn the boat in the fog: Life's
dense nothingness. And row,
row.

Kolbein Falkeid,
from the poem 'Another Sun'

Contents

Foreword

The original working title for this book was *Soppdagelse*, a play on the Norwegian word for mushrooms and other fungi, *sopp*, and the word for discovery *oppdagelse*. So, this is an account of one anthropologist's journey of discovery into the world of mushrooms, and of my fascination with fungi and the mushroom gatherers I met along the way. My new interest in mycology brought joy and meaning to my life at a time when everything looked very dark. There is no doubt in my mind that it was this interest in mushrooms and mushroom trails which helped me to find my way back to life after the unexpected death of my husband. Some way into writing this book, I began to wonder where and how I could weave in a line or two about him. Should I mention his death in the foreword, perhaps? I sat down and started writing what would eventually become Chapter 2 ('The next best death'). From that moment on, the whole concept of this book changed completely; the link between my exploration of the world of fungi and my wandering through the wilderness of grief seemed to be the most interesting story here. So this book tells of two parallel journeys: an outer one, into the realm of mushrooms, and an inner one, through the landscape of mourning.

For me, there are certain phases of the writing process which are necessarily solitary, with long hours of working alone, and others where I am dependent on feedback from excellent helpers whom I trust. My thanks, therefore, to Aud Korbøl, Bente Helenesdatter Pettersen, Berit Berge, Gudleiv Forr, Hadia Tajik, Hanne Myrstad, Hanne Sogn, Klaus Høiland, Johs. Bøe, Jon Lidén, Jon Martinsen Strand, Jon Trygve Monsen, Lars Myrstad Kringen, Mari Finness, Nina Z. Jørstad and the Tidemannsstuen writers' group, Ole Jan Borgund, Oliver Smith, Ottar Brox, Runar Kristiansen, and Åsta Øvregaard for their input. Thank you all for invaluable assistance and stimulating conversations! Many thanks also to my sources in mycology circles, to the good people at Norwegian Ethnological Research (NEG) at the Norwegian Museum of Cultural History, and the Ethnographic Library, University of Oslo, for their kind and indispensable help. From the outset, the Norwegian Non-Fiction Authors and Translators Association provided a grant without which this book would not have been possible. I am also deeply grateful to Professors Leif Ryvarden and Gro Gulden for expert mycological advice.

This book is dedicated to the memory of my husband, in gratitude for all our wonderful years together.

Long Litt Woon
Rødelokken Allotments, May 2017

*One mushroom,
one delight
Two mushrooms,
double delight*

This is the story of a journey which started on the day when my life was turned upside down: the day when Eiolf went to work and didn't come home. He never came back. Life as I had known it was gone in that instant. The world would never be the same again.

I was devastated. The pain of my loss was all that was left of him. It tore me apart, but I had no wish to dull the agony with painkillers. I wanted to suffer every ounce of the torment, raw. It was confirmation that he had lived, that he had been my husband. I did not want that to be gone as well.

I was in free fall. I, who had always been in command and in control; I, who liked to have a firm grip on things. My lodestar was gone. I found myself in unknown territory, a reluctant wanderer in a strange land. Visibility was poor and I had neither map nor compass. Which way was up, which way was down? From which corner should I start walking? Where should I set my foot?

There was nothing but blackness.

To my surprise, I chanced upon the answers to these questions where I least expected them.

The weather was damp, there was a light drizzle in the air, and the dead leaves that had fallen from the tall, venerable trees in Oslo's Botanical Gardens were starting to moulder. There was no doubt that the warm days of summer were over and a colder season was starting to encroach on our lives. Someone had told me about this course and I had signed up for it without giving it too much thought. It was something Eiolf and I had talked about doing, but never got round to. So, one autumn-dark evening I presented myself, not expecting too much, in the basement of the Natural History Museum at the University of Oslo.

I needed to watch my step: I had already managed to break an ankle just after Eiolf's funeral. The fear of falling remained with me long after the accident. I had been told that it takes a while for a broken ankle to heal, but whether a broken heart could ever be whole again and, if so, how long that might take, no one could tell me.

Grief grinds slowly: it devours all the time it needs.

The course of bereavement does not run smooth, it progresses in fits and starts, takes unforeseeable turns.

If anyone had told me that mushrooms would be my lifeline, the thing that would help me back onto my feet and quite literally back onto life's track, I would have rolled my eyes. What had mushrooms to do with mourning?

But it was out in the open woodland, on moss-covered ground, that I stumbled on what I was searching for. My exploration of the mushroom terrain also became a ramble through an inner landscape, a *via interna*. The outer journey has been time-consuming. So too has the inner journey, and it has also been turbulent and challenging. For me there is no doubt that my discovery of the realm of fungi steadily nudged me out of the tunnel of grief. It eased the pain and became my path out of the darkness. It offered me fresh perspectives and led me, little by little, to a new standpoint. Only later did it dawn on me that mushrooms had been my rescue in my hour of need, and that seemingly unrelated subjects such as mushrooms and mourning can, in fact, be connected. That is what this book is about.

I had better start, therefore, with the beginners' course on mushrooms.

Mushrooms for beginners

A lot of people had signed up for this course. Some in the flower of youth, others enjoying a second blooming. They came from all over the city; this was, it seemed, an interest shared by denizens of both the wealthier west side and the poorer east side of Oslo. As a social scientist, I find this interesting. We are inclined to associate certain sections of society with particular sports or hobbies. Some leisure pursuits have distinct middle-class overtones, others are seen as the province of different socio-economic groups. You don't have to be an anthropologist to discern this pattern in Oslo too, although Norwegians value their image as an egalitarian nation. Given the choice, Norwegians would pick the photograph of King Olav V buying a ticket on the electric train to the Holmenkollen ski slopes in 1973 as their country's profile picture. And even though it is true that few other monarchs have ever travelled by public transport, it is also the case that the Norwegian royal family is not generally given to taking the bus or the train.

There was something classless about the mushroom community that immediately appealed to me. I've been one of their number for some time now, yet I still don't know what the mushroomers I meet do in their day-to-day lives. Talk of fungi crowds out everything else. Trivial matters such as religion and politics have to take a back seat. Not that there isn't a hierarchy among mushroom enthusiasts: this field, too, has its heroes and villains, its unwritten rules and its conflicts, with plenty of scope for feelings to run high. Like all other communities, mushroom pickers represent a microcosm of society as a whole, although I didn't see this to begin with.

Mushrooms induce in us both fascination and fear: they lure us with the promise of sensual delights, but the threat of deadly poison lurks in the background. Not only that, certain species grow in fairy rings and others have hallucinogenic properties. Delve into historical sources and you will find that, through the ages, people have always been fascinated by fungi: they have no roots, no visible seeds, and yet they will suddenly spring up, often after heavy rain and thunderstorms, almost like an incarnation of the untamed forces of nature. The folk names for some fungi — Witch's Egg, Devil's Urn, or Jack o' Lantern, for example — suggest that mushrooms were once seen as having a whiff of paganism about them, of being uncanny, magical.

For some, an interest in fungi is sparked by a fascination with the function of mushrooms as the recyclers of the eco-system. Others are more interested in their medicinal properties. There is a lot of optimism surrounding research into the uses of mushrooms in the treatment of cancer. Norway has made its own contribution to medical science with the Cyclosporin fungus, *Tolypocladium inflatum,* found on the Hardangervidda plateau, an extract from which forms the basis of an indispens-able drug used in organ transplantation. Those who imagine that mushrooms can work wonders as aphrodisiacs munch the phallic Common Stinkhorn, *Phallus impudicus,* or the equally priapic Dog Stinkhorn, *Mutinus ravenelii.* Handcraft enthusiasts have embraced fungi as new and exciting sources of dyes for wool, linen, and silk. For nature photographers, fungi present a riotous cornucopia: mushrooms come not only in brown and white, but in every imaginable, and unimaginable, shape and hue. They may be stubby and springy, lovely and graceful, delicate and transparent, or so spectacular and bizarre that they seem like something from another planet. Some are even luminescent and can light up a forest path when darkness falls.

However, most of the people I know who are interested in learning about picking wild mushrooms do so because they enjoy eating them. Despite determined efforts, commercial growers have still not succeeded in farming the most sought after mushrooms. So fungi could be said to provide the perfect antithesis to the regimented world in which most of us live. 'Can you eat it?' is the question which the majority of those who don't know much about mushrooms ask again and again.

The antiquated name of the body running the course had piqued my interest: The Greater Oslo Fungi and Useful Plants Society — it sounded like a sister organisation to the Norwegian Women's Hygiene Association. What sort of people got involved with fungi and useful plants? To be honest, I wasn't sure what constituted a useful plant. And if you pursued that line of thought: what about useless plants? Was there a society for them as well? I didn't dare ask this question in front of everyone else.

The leader of the course had a knife in a leather sheath at his belt and a small magnifying glass hanging from a cord around his neck: both these items form an essential part of the serious mushroom forager's uniform, although I didn't know that then. Style, I would learn, is not high on a mushroomer's list of priorities. When you go hunting in the forest your clothing has to be practical and functional. Which is why, at first glance, mushroom gatherers can look like something from another planet, clad top to toe in waterproofs and slathered in lotions to ward off mosquitoes, midges, and deer flies.

'So, what are mushrooms?' the course leader asked. Many of the class members said nothing and tried to avoid the teacher's eye. As did I. Surely that was obvious; everybody knew what a mushroom was. But the teacher was looking for a more scientific answer and I had no idea where to start looking for such a thing.

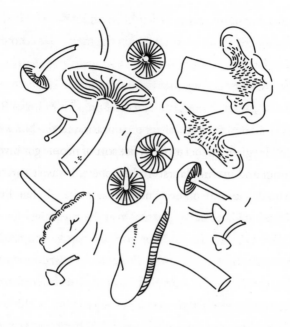

What many people, myself included, think of when they think of mushrooms are in fact just some of the fungi of the world of mycology. Mycology is the study of fungi. Most species of fungi are much smaller than the mushrooms we know, often microscopic. I am frequently asked how many different species of mushroom there are, but the world of fungi is so vast that it is hard to say for sure. The question of the number of fungi yet to be discovered and scientifically documented is a serious bone of contention among experts in the field. Some experts say two million. Others, five million. The Natural History Museum at the University of Oslo has attempted to produce a comprehensive record of all the different species found in Norway. Fungi account for almost 20 per cent of the nigh on 44,000 species recorded in the country. By comparison, mammals account for only 0.2 per cent.

The mushrooms one finds in the forest are only a tiny part of a much greater organism. The bulk of this is formed by a dynamic, living network of long, shoestring-like cells known as mycelium, which spread underground or through trees and other plants. What we see growing above ground is the mushroom's fruit, with the same relationship to the whole organism as an apple has to the apple tree, except that in this case the 'tree' grows below ground. The world's largest organism is a honey fungus: the Dark Honey Fungus, *Armillaria ostoyae*. It is found in the east of the American state of Oregon, where it covers a stretch of woodland corresponding to almost four square miles and is known colloquially as The Humongous Fungus. Hundreds of samples of this fungus have been taken, and analysis of the mycelium's DNA has shown that it all radiates from a single genetic individual, estimated to be between 2,000 and 8,000 years old. Above ground, the world's largest species of fungus is probably the African *Termitomyces titanicus*. Its cap can grow to over a metre in width. Looking at photographs of people in Africa holding specimens of this mushroom over their heads like umbrellas one could be forgiven for thinking that these images must have been manipulated.

We only see a mushroom for a very short period in its life cycle. The rest of the time it gets on with its life well hidden from us. When conditions are right, wild mushrooms drive upwards from the mycelium network and break through the soil with a force that can lift rocks and split tarmac. From the course leader, we learned that, far from growing only in forests, mushrooms also spring up in public parks, by the roadside, and even in graveyards and private gardens. Fungi flourish everywhere, if we are to go by the fungi aficionados, who don't merely believe that where there is life there are mushrooms, as well as hope, but who will even go so far as to claim that fungi are essential to existence: no fungi, no life. In fact, there is a video — one that is forever being referred to in mushrooming circles — explaining how fungi could save the world.[1] They are strong in their faith, these mushroomers.

All good teachers will start by establishing how much their pupils know. So why not kick off the course with a quiz on the best known mushrooms? The aim of this course for beginners was to teach us how to recognise about 15 different species of fungi. Fresh specimens which had, only a few hours earlier, been living peacefully in quiet forests, had been ripped out of their sleepy existence in the moist earth to be employed as educational tools, passed round in class, one after the other. I felt the fear of being the class dunce well up inside me. Of the mushrooms handed to me, the only one I recognised was the chanterelle, the golden beauty of the forest. Clearly, there was plenty to be learned here.

In the past, I later discovered, fungi posed a serious head-ache for science. Even Carl von Linné (1707-1778) — known as the father of modern taxonomy for his creation of a system for the classification of every species of animal and plant, a system still used to this day — struggled with fungi. In the Linneaen system, they ended up in a sub-category of the animal kingdom entitled 'Chaos'. It was almost as if the usual laws of nature did not apply to them. Since then, however, it has been established that fungi belong neither to the plant kingdom nor the animal kingdom, they form their *own* kingdom. The fungi kingdom.

This was news to me. I had simply assumed that mushrooms were a weird sort of plant. We also learned that the members of the fungi kingdom are more closely akin to those of the animal kingdom and, consequently, to *Homo sapiens*, than to the plant kingdom! Hence the reason that extracts from fungi are used in human medicine: in vital antibiotics, such as penicillin, for example, and drugs used in the treatment of cancer. Now there's something they didn't teach us in biology lessons in Malaysia. In the biology classroom at the girls' school I attended hung large wall-charts showing illustrations of plants with the names of their various parts written in elegant copperplate. I had been given something to think about next time I picked up my distant relative the button mushroom in the supermarket.

Our first lesson dealt with the proper picking technique: we were instructed to take hold of the mushroom just where the stem, or stipe, left the soil and grip it firmly while we gently eased the mushroom out. It is handy to have a knife with you, since mushrooms sometimes lie hidden deep in the carpet of moss or stubbornly refuse to budge. A small brush is another good thing to have, a pastry brush, say, or an old toothbrush, for some first rough field cleaning, something which is strongly recommended since it cuts down cleaning and preparation time

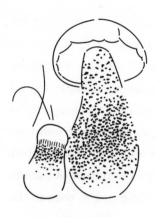

Leccinum versipelle,
Orange Birch Bolete

at home considerably. Apparently, though, there are those who find cleaning mushrooms a meditative process.

The first thing to do when you find a mushroom is to check how it looks under its cap. What you see under the cap can provide relevant information for determining which species a particular specimen belongs to; for example, whether it is a member of the bolete, tooth, polypore, or gilled fungi — all groups covered by the beginners' course. Once you know the answer to this question, the next thing is to ascertain which genus it belongs to, and then which species you have in your hand.

First, we were handed a real live bolete fungus — an Orange Birch Bolete, *Leccinum versipelle.* One of the main distinguishing features of bolete fungi is the underside of the cap, which both looks and feels like a sponge. We learned that no bolete fungus native to Norway is poisonous once it has been heated, a fact which was carefully noted by everyone. This soft, spongy mushroom feels weird to the touch and reacts oddly too. Fingertip pressure on the pore surface can alter the colour of some bolete fungi, causing them to turn blue. This tendency to 'bruise' is one way of identifying certain species. Although today I can recognise an Orange Birch Bolete a mile off, without pressing the pore surface, it is still tempting to do so. There is a childish glee to be had from seeing the mushroom turn blue.

When I was a child in Malaysia, we would spend hours playing with a plant that drew in its leaves and closed up whenever it was touched. We would then wait patiently for it to open — so that we could touch it again. The same procedure every time, but we never tired of it. On the contrary, we thought it was great fun. Since then I have discovered that this plant is called *Mimosa pudica* and that *pudica* is the Latin word for 'shy'. It is usually found in shady spots, under trees or bushes. The Norwegian Orange Birch Bolete reminds me a little of this Malaysian plant. Nature seems almost to be communicating and playing with us in a simple, wordless dialogue.

We were also introduced to tooth fungi, which have 'teeth' or 'spines' on their underside. The species *Hydnum repandum* is known in English as the Hedgehog Mushroom. Some people scrape off the spines before cooking the mushrooms because loose spines can look like little white larvae in the pan. But this is just an optical illusion. The Hedgehog Mushroom was one of our course leader's 'five safe mushrooms', which is to say edible mushrooms that have no sinister lookalikes. It was the first time I had heard the term 'safe mushrooms'. These I would have to remember.

The course also covered the polypores. The Sheep Polypore, *Albatrellus ovinus*, another of the five safe mushrooms, belongs to this group. The Sheep Polypore has a rather deformed and lumpy appearance. If you turn it upside down, the underside

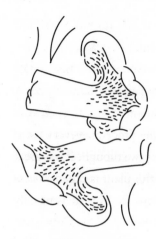

Hydnum repandum,
Hedgehog Mushroom

looks like a pincushion with lots of holes pricked in it. When cooked, the Sheep Polypore changes colour, from white to lemony yellow. The colour change undergone by some species when heated is an important detail, since it provides another key to the identity of a mushroom. The Orange Birch Bolete, to which we had already been introduced, also changes colour when heated, from white to dark blue. The world of fungi was unquestionably even stranger than I had imagined when I walked into that class.

Among the gilled fungi are found many genera of mushrooms, including the most dangerous and the tastiest. As a beginner, it was therefore important to learn to recognise the most common. Russulas are members of the gilled fungi group and are often very brightly coloured. They could be said to be the flowers of the mushroom world, coming as they do in so many vivid tones of red, purple, yellow, grey, blue, and green. The very name 'Russula' is enough to make the mouth water. The etymological dictionary suggests that the Norwegian word for Russula, *kremle*, may be related to the dialect word *krembel*, meaning 'small or fat thing', which is a pretty good description of Russulas in general. Like all gilled fungi, milk caps also have gills and exude a milky fluid when cut. The milk of some milk caps is actually coloured; the Saffron Milk Cap, *Lactarius delicio-sus*, and the Orange Milk Cap, *Lactarius deterrimus*, which have carroty red milk, we were told, are among the five safe mush-rooms. I saw now that this was a far more colourful world than I had thought. Although there are many theories, no one knows why these mushrooms come in so many colours. There was a lot more to mushrooms, it seemed, than the bland off-white or dirty-brown mushrooms, *Agaricus bisporus*, sold alongside the tomatoes and cucumbers in supermarkets.

My interest was piqued, in particular, by another gilled fungi, various edible *Agaricus* species found in the wild. We were told that these tasted much, much better than the standard supermarket mushroom, a farmed *Agaricus*, but that this genus can be a rather tricky one for beginners. For one thing, it has been known for individuals to confuse edible *Agaricus* species with poisonous lookalikes. I was very keen to discover how these wild *Agaricus* mushrooms tasted. And whether I would ever be able to tell the various different species apart. I jotted down notes as fast as I could and had soon filled several pages.

In addition to edible mushrooms, the course syllabus also included the main toxic fungi. The Roman emperor Tiberius Claudius was poisoned by mushrooms served to him by his own wife, Agrippina, in 54 A.D. Not surprisingly, the whole class found this subject most intriguing. The toadstool familiar from fairy tales, Fly Agaric or *Amanita muscaria*, which is also a fixture of Norwegian Christmas decorations, is a poisonous mushroom, but not nearly as toxic as the deadliest fungi found in Norway. The Destroying Angel, *Amanita virosa*, is a snow-white mushroom with a slender stem with what is known as a 'ring' around it, and, unlike the Fly Agaric, it is deadly poisonous. Some Asian immigrants to Norway have learned the hard way that the Angel's snowy beauty is deceptive. Unfortunately, this mushroom looks disconcertingly like another mushroom which is regarded as a delicacy in Asia, the *Amanita chepangiana*, which many immigrants from that part of the world know of from home.

Another poisonous mushroom we were told to watch out for was the Death Cap, *Amanita phalloides*. This mushroom is reported to have a mild and not unpleasant taste. As with the Destroying Angel, ingestion of it can be fatal. But how do we know that this mushroom is mild tasting when it is deadly? No one asked this question; instead we all sat in awed silence.

As a simple rule of thumb, we novices were admonished to avoid any wild mushrooms which were entirely white or entirely brown, i.e. on the cap, the underside, and the stem. Other than that, the two course leaders had no simple rules to offer us. We realised that there was no easy way of knowing whether a mushroom was poisonous or not. Mushrooms simply have to be learned, one by one. Full stop. Our teachers were very clear on this point.

I was astonished to find that the popular chanterelle was not included in any of the individual course leaders' own five favourite mushrooms. Their ideal mushroom might, for example, be the Sheathed Woodtuft, the Horn of Plenty, the Penny Bun, the Saffron Milk Cap, the Prince mushroom, the Tawny Milk Cap, or the true morel. The chanterelle's less well-known cousins had names straight out of a fairy tale. They seemed both familiar and alien. If one reeled them off one after another it sounded a little like a piece of modern poetry, where nothing rhymed but where, for just a nano-second, you felt you were on the brink of understanding something. The chanterelle, *Cantharellus cibarius*, is a mushroom with a funnel-shaped cap, as its genus name, *Cantharellus*, meaning 'little goblet', suggests. Unlike most other popular mushrooms, with its golden apricot colour the chanterelle cries out to be found. For those who enjoy a more challenging hunt, chanterelles are almost too easy to discover. Later, I was to get to know mushroom pickers who would walk straight past 'ordinary' chanterelles in the forest. And if the chanterelle were mentioned, it was almost apologetically ('Oh, of course, chanterelles are all right every now and again.'). Compared to other mushrooms, the chanterelle also has a long season. In Norway the first ones appear as early as June, a secret which mushroomers keep to themselves.

What was it that mushroom enthusiasts knew about these other mushrooms that I, a novice, was, with any luck, on the verge of discovering for myself?

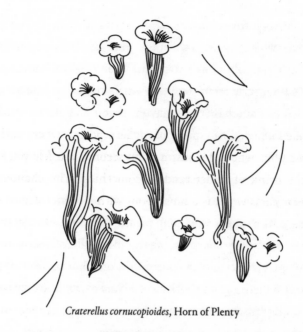

Craterellus cornucopioides, Horn of Plenty

The adrenalin rush

After an evening of theory, the next item on the programme was a field trip. In Norway, outdoor life is tantamount to a religion, and Sunday outings in the hills or the forest are almost obligatory. For an outsider, though, such an outing can be anything but a walk in the park. To the uninitiated, the forest can be a daunting place. It is alarming to discover, when the same clump of mushrooms shows up for the second time, that you have simply been going round in circles. It is very easy, I find, to be lured deeper and deeper into the dark forest and suddenly find one's self alone and surrounded by huge trees, with no obvious way back. At such times it is not hard to imagine that you can hear the trees whispering to one another that they are going to catch this little mushroom gatherer with their long branches. It's an ominous scenario for anyone who wasn't born with hiking boots on their feet and hasn't been taught that a walk in the woods is the best cure for a bad mood. In Malaysia, the tropical rainforest is not a place for Sunday outings. The concept is unknown there. And if anyone were mad enough to do such a thing, they would have to go armed with both mosquito repellent and a sharp *parang* — at the very least. But no one does this, because it is a dangerous activity, one involving risk to both life and limb. So the Norwegian tradition of getting out into the great outdoors had come as something of a shock to me. No one taught us expectant young people from all over the world, on an exchange year in the country, how to crack the Norwegian forest and mountain code. I had to figure it out for myself, stretching my comfort zone in the process. So it was good to go mushroom picking in a forest with our two course leaders, both of them certified mushroom professionals and well used to walking in the Norwegian forests. I couldn't help giggling the first time I heard the term 'certified mushroom professionals'. Prior to that, I had only ever heard the word professional used in connection with scientific, academic, or legal matters. It had never occurred to me that you could also be a professional in something like mushrooms.

On organised field trips, one learns how the appearance of different species of fungi changes *in situ*, from pinheads to full-grown mushroom. Some books on fungi only contain illustrations of perfect, fully grown specimens, which is no help when it comes to knowing how these mushrooms look at all of the different stages in their life cycle. Time takes its toll on everyone and everything, including mushrooms.

How did I become hooked on mushrooms? This question can be answered with a story from my very first mushroom hunt with the teachers from the beginners' course. Just after we entered the forest, I spotted a clump of eight or nine Destroying Angels. They looked so virginal and innocent, but still I went cold inside at the sight of these deadly mushrooms. It was incredible to be able to use my newly acquired skills straight away. Knowing what not to eat from the wild made me feel a little more familiar with this difficult subject. A warm thrill of achievement ran through me. And then I found some Horn of Plenty, well camouflaged by dead leaves and twigs, a delicacy new to me, which was identified by the course leader. I was a little surprised because these mushrooms were grey and black in colour and, to my mind back then, did not look like something one would eat. Which just goes to show how wrong you can be when you are working with preconceived notions based on assumptions and not on knowledge. Never before had I taken a course from which the lessons learned could immediately be put into practice, and I was extremely impressed by the teachers from The Greater Oslo Fungi and Useful Plants Society. I went home with a basket full of edible mushrooms, pleased as Punch with my haul and with myself.

As I became more familiar with the main genera of mushrooms, I gained a slightly more structured view of the complex fungi kingdom. Maybe one day I would feel confident about identifying the 15 species covered on the course. The syllabus for Norway's so-called mushroom inspector's exam covered at least 150 species. But how was one ever to become fully conversant in 150 species when it was hard enough recognising just 15? It seemed an absolutely impossible task.

A walk through the woods is a very different experience when undertaken armed with new knowledge, however limited it may be. Suddenly I was seeing mushrooms everywhere, fungi that I would simply have walked past before, blending as they did into the landscape. Now they were popping out at me in 3D, as if I had been given special glasses with which to see them. I also learned a lot about Norwegian flora — such as the fact that blue wood anemones are lime-loving plants. If I come across blue wood anemones there is a good chance that nearby I'll also find mushrooms which thrive in lime-rich soil.

Once I had recognised my first mushrooms, the exotic Norwegian woodlands began to make more sense to me. As time went on, I found myself longing to go there, to those dark-green forests. Nowadays, I scan the forest floor to gain a quick overview of the terrain as I walk along. Are there any interesting specimens here, I wonder? If you want to find mushrooms you have to turn off your mobile phone, switch to mushroom mode, and simply be there — in the woods. Since then, I have read that a walk in the woods can do wonders, not just for body and soul as the outdoor evangelists preach, but also for the brain.

As children, we have all known what it is to be fascinated

by something: to be so lost in watching ants hard at work, for example, that you don't hear the call for dinner. The mushroom adventure is every bit as spellbinding. You switch off from all the day-to-day trivia on a mushroom hunt. The hunter-gatherer instinct is kindled and you are instantly transported into a unique enchanted world. The concentration is sharpened and the tension mounts: will I find that mushroom treasure or not? And when they do finally come upon a swish chanterelle or two or three, a person is liable to catch themselves exclaiming 'Oh, gosh, aren't you gorgeous!' or even 'Come to mamma, darling!' But often I would be fooled by a yellow birch leaf which, for a moment, made my heart beat a little faster at the thought of possibly finding gold in the greenwood. Usually it proves to be neither gold nor mushroom, although on one occasion my laser gaze did spot some stray banknotes in the middle of a pinewood. It's amazing what you can find in a Norwegian forest if you just keep your eyes open.

Athletes talk about 'flow', the sense of control achieved when there is a balance between skills and challenges. When they are entirely immersed in the moment and the body is in tune with the activity, mind and spirit are bombarded by positive impulses. With focus and fixity of purpose come joy and excitement. Then they are 'in the zone'. In the East, the term 'Zen moment' has long been used for what happens when, after much practice, you are able to give yourself up to the experience of existential timelessness and placelessness. In many ways, flow and Zen are related experiences. You are contained within a bubble of happiness. The world can go on without you.

Unlike the athletes' sense of flow and the monks' Zen moment, the joys of mushroom picking were something I experienced while still new to the game, without any of sport's obligatory 10,000 hours of training or the Zen monk's rituals under my belt. I'm sure that skiing, sailing, and other sports and hobbies call for a lot more basic training before one can hope to experience a similar high. But when it comes to mushrooms you don't need any great skill to feel that rush of adrenalin. All you have to do to experience the thrill of mushroom hunting is to take a little walk with a mushroom expert. The mushroom high is easily won, a sort of 'flow light'.

Since I became bitten by the mushroom bug, I have discovered an invisible, parallel world right at my feet, one with its own unruly logic and wayward vitality, a magical world which I would once have walked straight past, unwitting. Sometimes, when I find mushrooms, time seems to stand still. I experience both flow and Zen. The sense of gratification and of being at one with the universe bring both inner contentment and happiness. At such moments only one thing matters: to be exactly where I am and do exactly what I am doing. At such moments I don't think about what I'm going to have for dinner or what people think of my hairstyle.

Gathering mushrooms is both a tactile and a sensory experience. First you feel the degree of resistance in the mushroom.

Some stubborn fungi dig in their heels, others are ready to leave the forest and come home with us if we merely smile sweetly at them. I love the moment when, after a little careful grubbing about, I finally have my golden prize in my hand. To me it feels almost like scraping my way to the winning number on a scratch card, a cheap thrill in more ways than one.

One thing is the sense of mastery that comes with more knowledge and more practice in exploring a forest. Something else, and quite unexpected, is the feeling of euphoria: my heart leapt the first time I found a delicious edible mushroom on my own. Was this happiness? It was staggering to actually feel an emotion I thought had gone for good when Eiolf died. It was like being given an intravenous shot of multi-vitamins. What a sensation! Elation bubbled out of every cell in my body. All at once a slender, golden beam of light pierced my soul. Was it possible to feel a delight so scintillatingly clear when everything seemed so vague and hopeless?

Find one mushroom and there's a good chance that you will find another nearby. The thrill of discovery is cumulative: one mushroom, one delight; two mushrooms, double delight.

As the world of mushrooms opened up to me, I began to see that the path back to life was easier than I had thought. It was simply a matter of gathering delights that flash and sparkle. All I had to do was follow the mushroom trail, even though I still didn't know where it would lead. What would I find in the great unknown that lay ahead of me? What lay beyond those hilltops and mists and turns in the road?

The next
best death

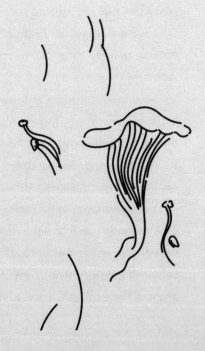

Death came for Eiolf early one bright summer morning. Before he had got as far as his office. Before he had got as far as putting on the water for his coffee and dumping his heavy shoulder bag. As usual, he was one of the first to arrive. It was the last time he would ever go to work, but how could we have known that? This man, at the midpoint of his life. Or so we thought.

Eiolf died suddenly. So suddenly that I still wonder whether he was aware of what was happening. Did he realise that this was it, that his allotted span had run out? Did he understand that he had reached the farthest shore? What was his last thought? Was death as he had imagined it would be? Was he drawn, slowly and surely, towards a brilliant light? Was the radiance of that light warm and intense, like being in love, like one of the most wonderful experiences anyone can have?

Fortunately, a few other people had also come in early that morning. One of his colleagues saw Eiolf fall. At first he thought he had just tripped, but he very quickly realised that something was seriously wrong. Once Eiolf had been driven away in the ambulance, this colleague called me. I was awake, just out of the shower, and about to start the day with a leisurely breakfast. Before I'd had a chance to digest this absurd message the telephone rang again.

The voice on the other end was not one I knew. It was the doctor from the hospital. I was still a bit dazed by the first call from Eiolf's colleague.

'I'm afraid I have bad news,' the doctor said.

My heart froze.

'Your husband is dead. I'm so sorry,' the doctor went on, steady as a metronome.

Out of the blue, word of his death hurled slap in my face.

'How? What? —' I scarcely remember what I said.

'Your husband lost consciousness immediately. He didn't feel a thing,' the doctor said.

I said nothing. I didn't know what questions to ask.

'It's the best death any of us could wish for,' he added.

I felt a wave of protest rise up inside me and stick in my throat. I didn't agree, not at all, but I found it impossible to speak. The doctor may have been trying to comfort me by saying this. But I was in no mood for bureaucratic solace. I am firmly convinced that the very best way to die would be to be fully conscious, without any acute pain, and to be granted a period of grace in which to say a proper goodbye. It isn't only one's nearest and dearest who need this. The person departing this life needs it too. Concluding a life takes time.

I felt as though someone had whacked me with a massive sledgehammer, the heaviest there is. The room was spinning.

I had to sit down. I broke out in a cold sweat. Inside me, chaos reigned, a state of emergency had been declared. I felt sick. Was I dreaming or was I awake? How can he be dead, this man who I had always expected to outlive me? Only a few hours earlier, there had been two of us, sharing a life. It had always been us two, ever since I was 18 and Eiolf was 21. Now he was in the emergency unit at Ullevål Hospital. Dead. So alive one moment. So dead the next. Only a heartbeat separating the one state from the other. My best friend was gone. I was alone in the world.

I didn't want to hang up the phone; I pressed it even harder to my ear. I wanted the doctor to go on talking. No detail would be too small. Everything he could tell me about Eiolf was of the greatest interest. The doctor was my only link to the brutal fact that had skewered me that morning. I think I may have forgotten to breathe. Eiolf was the reason I had changed my plans for my adult life and moved to Norway from Malaysia. I would never see him again, never speak to him, smell him, hold him. It made no sense. That telephone call had sliced my life in two. By the time I hung up the phone my old life was no more.

Any long marriage has only two possible endings: divorce or death. Ours ended when Eiolf died. Death is absolute: either you're dead or you're not. What separates the one state from the other are a myriad slender, transparent threads. Sometimes these threads are supple, sturdy, and strong, and prevent one from crossing over to the land of the dead. We've all heard stories of individuals who cheat death, who are saved at the last moment, against all the odds. Almost every day you read of such miracles in the tabloids. But sometimes the threads are delicate and fragile. They fall apart and crumble away to nothing if you so much as look at them. Then the path from life to death is brutally short. Then you step off the knife-edge of life and are gone. And there's no way back.

They were waiting for me. They knew who I was there to see. But I wasn't allowed to go to Eiolf straight away. First, a nurse took me into an office to have a word with me. I think they wanted to prepare me and calm me down. I was handed some cold water in a plain paper cup. I drank the water without giving any thought to whether I was thirsty or not. After a little chat the nurse asked me to follow her. We walked along some corridors and stopped in front of a door on the same floor. She opened the door, and there lay my husband, under a duvet, for all the world as if he were asleep. Even though I'd known we were going to see Eiolf I was surprised to suddenly come upon him there. The bed linen was fresh, there were flowers and lit candles. The room had an air of solemnity about it, one which spoke of a reverence for death, and for life.

I had imagined having to go down into a cold, dark basement. I had pictured Eiolf lying all alone on a cold steel trolley, with a sheet pulled up over his face. But here he was, as if asleep, so peaceful in a newly made bed. My legs gave way and I collapsed into an untidy heap on the floor. I was shaking all over. I could hear my pulse pounding fit to burst. Again and again I begged Eiolf to wake up, but he made no response. The nurse averted her eyes, perhaps to give me some privacy at this agonising moment? But I didn't care about her. I wanted so much to hold him and touch him. I ran my hand over the smooth sheet under the duvet and rested it on him. He was still warm! That I hadn't expected. I felt a sudden flush of gratitude. He had waited for me! I had managed to get to him before he grew dead-cold and unreachable.

Although I knew Eiolf was dead, it was still hard to comprehend. Maybe the doctors had got it all wrong. Maybe the age of miracles wasn't past. Maybe he would wake up and smile. Maybe next time I blinked he would slowly open his eyes, look at me, and say one of those things that only he could say.

I blinked. He didn't wake up. Life stood still. There was nothing for it but to bury my last mad shred of hope.

When I finally left the hospital, I carried away with me two plastic bags containing his clothes and his shoulder bag. In his bag was his camera, which he always had with him. Eiolf loved taking photographs. It was strange to look at the subjects that had caught his eye for the last time, but I had no time to dwell on this.

There were umpteen practical questions to be answered. Which coffin? Burial or cremation? What date? What time? Which funeral chapel? What to say in the death notice? In the order of service? Which music should we choose? Who had to be informed? I was in pieces, but I had to see to things, make decisions.

I was working on auto-pilot. The phone never stopped ringing. No one could believe it. I was in shock, but I had to comfort and support others. I heard words issuing from my mouth, but had no idea where they were coming from. The days raced by. As if the fast forward button had got stuck. Where I was to be found in this frantic whirl is hard to say.

What took the greatest toll on me was something that I myself had decided on. I wanted to dress Eiolf before we put him in the coffin. When I mentioned this at the funeral home the undertaker didn't turn a hair. Anything was possible. At the funeral home you are presented with a long list of options and you quickly discover lots of needs you did not know you had. In Malaysia it is quite normal for the close family to wash and dress the deceased. And although I had never previously had occasion to do this, dressing Eiolf before we laid him in his coffin was something I knew I had to do myself. I also badly needed to see him, even though he was dead. I grew up with this tradition and I do not understand how relatives can leave everything to the undertakers, to meet the deceased again only when he or she is laid out in a closed coffin.

When I arrived at the hospital chapel at the agreed time, I was given the chance to change my mind. It was explained to me that I might find it hard because Eiolf had undergone a post-mortem. I was warned that this had left a large scar. A huge Y on the front of his body. Could a little more knowledge about the cause of death shed light on Eiolf's unexpected death? It was this possibility that had persuaded me to consent to it. But the post-mortem revealed no new or noteworthy details, nothing we didn't already know. So as far as Eiolf was concerned, the whole exercise had been a waste of time. Or had it been more for us, the bereaved? When I was ready, Eiolf was wheeled into the chapel. Or maybe he was already there in the room and was simply wheeled forward? I'm not quite sure, but I have a clear picture of his body being covered by a sheet. Not his face, though — I was happy about that.

The hospital chapel staff were right. I found it very hard to look at Eiolf. Not because of the incision that ran from his throat to his navel, sewn up with big, hasty stitches. But because he looked so dead. The skin of his face was so lifeless, soulless. Although he had been dead for some days I wasn't prepared for this. It was him and it wasn't him. It wasn't Eiolf we were looking at, but his body. The term 'death mask' acquired new meaning. How do you say goodbye when a life is definitively over? It must have been so cold, lying there naked on that narrow metal trolley. The post-mortem seemed to me to have removed the last vestiges of life from his body. He was no longer sleeping. He was blue with cold, and dead. Really dead. Now I knew for sure that he was beyond the reach of hope. But it was also good to see him again. He looked relaxed and peaceful. Both strong and vulnerable. Was that a faint smile on his lips?

The chapel was flooded with light from a large skylight. Several candles were also burning. A piece of modern stained-glass hung behind the trolley. Everything was clean and neat and peaceful. The surroundings were simple, not fancy or fussy. Almost elegant. I liked it. I stroked his cheek, as if to comfort him, even though he was past comforting. Or was it myself I was trying to comfort? The contrast to the task before me was stark. We were to dress Eiolf and lay him in his coffin. I was determined to be with him on this last stage of his journey. Life doesn't end in a single moment, with one last gasp for breath. Death is made up of thousands of little moments, divine in their banality. They are so precious and I treasure every one of them.

What should Eiolf wear? With us we had brought a relatively new, dark suit. We had also brought a new, gaily coloured sarong that my mother wanted to place in his coffin as a final tribute. The undertakers had brought a loose white smock of the sort often used for Norwegian funerals and a light, thin, white 'duvet'. It was a shock for me to discover that it was normal in Norway for the deceased to be left naked from the waist down. The 'duvet' laid over the smock created the illusion of slumber and a fully clothed corpse. Eiolf ended up in a white Norwegian smock and a colourful batik sarong from Malaysia, a long, ankle-length skirt. He always wore a sarong at home — the first thing he did when he got home from work was to change into one. He had no make-believe duvet over him in the coffin. Despite the lack of planning, the end result was pretty good. Almost beautiful, even. I was pleased that we had come up with an outfit for Eiolf that reflected the life he had led. It was good to know that we had managed to add a personal touch to a concrete task, that we hadn't simply taken the pre-packaged option from the funeral home's menu. We can find comfort and solace in the slightest details and the most unexpected places. But there is something final about closing the lid of a coffin. It underlines the fact that a life is definitely over.

There were a lot of people at the funeral, some known to me, others not. Eiolf's colleagues from work. Friends from university. Acquaintances from his life outside of work. Fellow allotment owners whom we used to see from May to October every year when we moved from our apartment to our summer cottage. Distant relatives with whom we were not in regular contact. It was strange to see the outlines of a life I thought I knew so well.

How do you say goodbye for the very last time? What do you say? I remember waking up far too early on the day before relatives were due to fly in from all the corners of the world. Eiolf was very much loved in our family home. My father always used to call him his 'favourite son-in-law'. Since I was his only daughter this was a family joke that was not only true, but which my father could repeat without offending his daughters-in-law. It was already a bright summer morning, although the whole town was still asleep. I woke up slowly and realised that I had dreamt of Eiolf! Oh, what bliss! It was unexpected, breathtaking. There was something angel-like about him now, he could come and go as he pleased. I opened my eyes and was immediately on the alert. Was Eiolf here, in the bedroom? Suddenly the words came to me. I picked up my pen and wrote the whole eulogy while still in bed.

Normally, I have no problem speaking to a large audience, so I shouldn't have been worried about giving my speech, but I still wasn't sure whether I would be able to get through what, to my mind, would have to stand as the performance of my life. Would I manage to stay upright and not crumple up in a heap? Would I manage to get the words out? My only consolation was that there was nothing I had left unsaid to Eiolf. I had counted myself lucky to have him as my husband and had had little to contribute when my women friends complained about their husbands in those routine female rituals. And luckily I had often told him so. It was a relief to know that I had also thanked him for letting me be myself in our marriage, and not a wife with room for improvement.

After the funeral, family, friends, and close acquaintances were invited back to the allotment association clubhouse. The menu was shockingly simple. No dainty canapés. No elaborate smørbrød, just hot-dog sausages and lomper — Norwegian potato pancakes. I had had to concentrate my energies on getting through the funeral. And the eulogy. I had given no thought whatsoever to what we should have to eat at the reception afterwards. I had a minor panic when it dawned on me that that, too, had to be organised. Then I had the idea for the sausages and promptly decided that that would have to do. It was actually a menu after Eiolf's own heart. Over the years he must have eaten any number of sausages wrapped in lomper that I didn't know about. Besides which, it would be easy to run out and buy more once we saw how many people showed up and how much was eaten. This appealed to my practical sensibilities.

U., a friend who had repeatedly offered to do anything he could to help, was given the job of hot-dog man. He asked how many people I thought would come. I couldn't say. I had no idea and was in no fit state to work it out. Nor do I remember who saw to the coffee. There were cakes, too. Where did they come from? Someone must simply have seen to that. Much of it was just a blur to me.

The clubhouse at the allotments provided the perfect setting for the wake. To get there you had to walk along the narrow paths between the rows of small wooden cottages, all with their own style, both in terms of the hut and the garden, in the unique Norwegian system of allotments with rustic but liveable cottages in the middle of the city. Some were pretty basic, others more elaborate. Some allotment holders have perfectly level, manicured lawns and monitor immaculate flower beds from minute to minute, while others go for a more rustic style, with plants and flowers allowed to flourish more freely. At the top of the path the landscape opens up. The clubhouse sits on a flat stretch of ground with a view of the little allotment cottages stretching out to either side. Eiolf would have liked to hear all the things that were said about him at the wake, but I think he would also have been a bit overwhelmed. He wasn't comfortable with being the centre of attention at social gatherings. Quiet by nature, he was nonetheless visible in his own way. But whatever our nature, a little praise does none of us any harm, if you ask me.

I think I must have collapsed after the funeral, fallen into a coma almost. When everything that had to be done had been done. When people who had come from near and far had gone home. When the flowers had withered and the phone stopped ringing. Sitting there alone in the flat with only my sad thoughts for company. That was when it really struck me that Eiolf would never come home from work again.

I went willingly into an inner exile. My sorrow swelled until it took over my life. I was swamped by grief: I woke in the morning, but had no desire to get up. I viewed the world through one single, solitary peephole, that of loss and pain. There was no place for me to hide. I could sob and wail all I liked, but the cold, hard fact was that no one answered. I laid my head on Eiolf's pillow. A deathly hush fell over our neighbourhood, Fagerborg.

The end of a great era in my life was a fact. Tormented, like Orpheus, I could find no obvious answer to the question: *What do I do without Eiolf?*

Everything that I had thought of as fixed and permanent, as solid load-bearing beams, had been turned into feather-light bubbles floating slowly away and vanishing from view. I was like the lightest of ping-pong balls, hurled into the ocean and tossed hither and yon on the swell. Grief is a stormy, shifting sea with no life buoy in sight. I was taken aback by the strength of the forces that pulled and tugged at me.

Life goes on, they say. But why do they say that when it is no help at all? Before one even begins to think about 'going on', as they say, one has to accept and absorb that the nightmare is real, that a life way beyond surreal is now a fact. How does one comprehend the incomprehensible?

I missed my old life. Was there a switch I could flick to turn back the clock?

I know it's all a matter of rebuilding one's life. In many ways it's a matter of surviving and living under another sun, but how was I to do that? Besides, as an immigrant who had stayed in this country because of a Norwegian, the following question now arose: *Should I go on living in this country?*

Of all the emotions, utter despair is the worst. One swings between desperation and madness so fast that everything is just a grey mush. The valley of despair is dry and barren. The road that stretched before me was remorseless. Was there something waiting at the other end? The signposts were unclear. The sun beats down as only it can and my rucksack is heavy as lead. My suffering is unbearable. There are no trees, and no shade to be found. Nothing but sharp stones all the way. For once, I envied the religious. Could it be that they are quicker to make sense of a death that seems so totally senseless? Could it be that the belief in eternal life makes it easier to live with the physical death?

Lots of people offer their condolences and their sympathy. I'm surrounded by good friends, but they can't bear this burden for me. Many people mourn for Eiolf, but my grief is mine and mine alone. It is my responsibility to turn suffocating sorrow into a pain that can be endured. It is up to me to get my life back onto an even keel.

There is only one thing to do, and that is to put one foot in front of the other and start walking, like a pilgrim wandering through an ancient landscape. Not much happens, but each day is, nonetheless, different. Life is static, even though I am in motion. Time both drags and flies by. It can be as long as the

Gobi Desert and short as an instant. I melt like a river flowing into the sea. I am the same, and yet different although I cannot explain how. Who am I now? I can't live the life I once had, but I don't know how my new life should be. To be honest, I don't really know what I'm looking for.

Eiolf was a great one for clowning and goofing around and he could always make me laugh. Would I ever laugh again?

He made me a better version of me. Now I would have to do that for myself. I wasn't sure if I would like me quite as much.

This was the start of the rest of my life, without Eiolf. My beloved's death had sent me off in a new direction, whether I liked it or not.

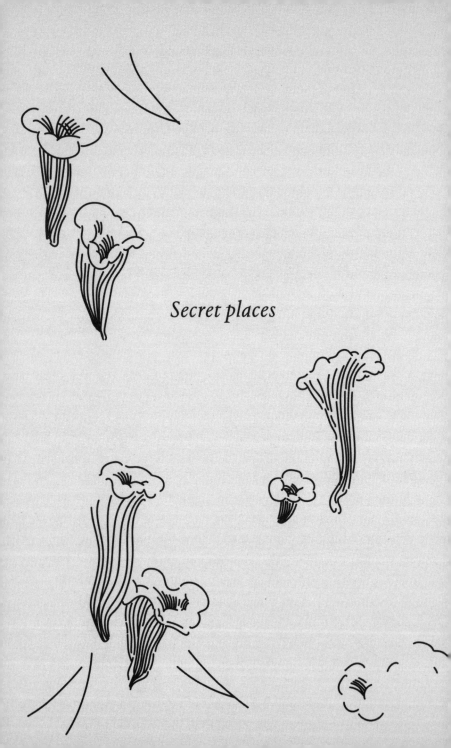

Secret places

Looking back on it, I can see that my grieving over Eiolf's death was similar in some ways to traditional anthropological field work. When working in the field an anthropologist lives with his informants in order to gain a better understanding of their life and culture from the inside. The early stages of a period of fieldwork tend to be rather chaotic, because there is so much one doesn't understand and one can easily become confused by all of the apparently contradictory impressions and explanations. Before the pieces of the puzzle can finally fall into place the anthropologist must develop, test, and reformulate working hypotheses for what initially seems incomprehensible.

So it was for me, as I tried to make sense of the senselessness that had hit me, with one big difference: this was no external, foreign world I was trying to decipher, but an internal, all-encompassing state of chaos. Who was I, now that my mate was gone? How was I to fill my life with new meaning? The fieldwork of the heart is a gruelling exercise.

The mushrooms I have learned to recognise have been like little rest areas, offering me sustenance and respite, before sending me on to the next staging post on this inner journey. The pleasure gained from my mushrooming forays has given me the incentive to immerse myself in the subject. Mushrooms provided me with a new perspective on things, not least when it came to making fresh sense of life. As I began to form a more structured picture of the seemingly bewildering fungi kingdom, so the fermentation of feelings inside me fell into some vague, loose sort of order.

But first I had to find mushrooms.

All beginners know that same frustration: in order to find mushrooms, first you have to know where to look. But, as everyone knows, the best mushroom sites are secret. Information on mushroom sites is in short supply and most mushroomers guard it as closely as their most precious jewels. One person I know has stored details of her best mushroom sites on her hand-held GPS tracker for her daughter to inherit. What chance did I have of finding the finest mushrooms when I didn't know anyone who would share their treasures with me?

In such a situation the best place to start is your local mycological society. On the society's forays, with their expert guides, you will be able to see fungi in their natural habitat and gradually learn to read the terrain. You don't learn where to look for mushrooms from reading a book at home with your feet up. Experienced mushroom foragers have an uncanny knack for spotting mushrooms. Even in an unfamiliar forest they always seem to know where to look. But there is no mystery to it. Over the years they have simply built up layer upon layer of knowledge — hands-on experience which is then systematically applied. I have gone foraging with older mushroom enthusiasts who wear glasses with very thick lenses but have a better eye for mushrooms than I do and will often spot mushrooms alongside the path after *I* have walked past them. They usually have a good chuckle about that. It's no good having youth on your side if you don't possess this sixth mushroom sense, this instinct for where best to look. The more experience you have, the more highly developed this sixth sense becomes. Some people even believe they can sniff out mushrooms in the forest, the way dogs and pigs can sniff out truffles, another greatly prized fungus.

I started going along on the open mushroom hunting expeditions organised by my own local society. These were always led by a certified mushroom professional, which was both reassuring and instructive. There were guided expeditions every weekend during the season. And sometimes on weekdays too. They took place in many places in Oslo that I, a long-time resident of the city, had never heard of. It was usually possible to get to the meeting point by public transport. Not only that, but these trips were free: a nice little gift from the society to the people of Oslo. One advantage of going on the society's organised expeditions is that you don't have to pay a visit to the mushroom inspectors afterwards. Such a visit can entail having to throw away all of your mushrooms because you've managed to slip one tiny, but deadly, mushroom in with the rest of the day's haul.

On the society's trips all the mushrooms picked are checked and discussed as they are found. Little by little, I began to draw up my own mental map of likely mushroom sites in Oslo. None of these places was secret, it's true, but they were all areas where I knew there was a good chance of finding mushrooms. You have to start somewhere.

Going mushroom hunting equipped with a mental map of likely sites is a very different matter from searching aimlessly for mushroom gold. I consider myself very fortunate to have been able to see, early in my 'mushroom career', how the real experts go about it. While on a visit to America I was invited on a private mushroom hunt in New York by no less a person than the late, great Gary Lincoff, former president of the North American Mycology Association and author of the American field bible, *National Audubon Society Field Guide to North American Mushrooms*.

Mushroom picking in New York's Central Park

Gary Lincoff, referred to by some as the Pied Piper of mushrooms, was a small man with a great sense of humour and a huge fund of knowledge. In his broad-brimmed hat and signature safari waistcoat he was a well-known figure at mycology conferences all over the world. We met as arranged in Central Park, said our hellos, and then, without any more ado, he began to march briskly and purposefully from one tree to another. I had to walk fast to keep up and not lose sight of my guide in one of New York's best hunting grounds.

To the uninitiated, Lincoff's hunting strategy might have seemed pretty random, but it was anything but. He had his regular trails around Central Park's 843 acres. Suddenly, he stopped and combed carefully through a patch of grass which didn't look as if it contained anything interesting at all. The grass was long. It had obviously been some time since the park-keepers had run the lawnmower over this spot. Then, *voilá*, Lincoff found what he was looking for: the edible Ringless Honey Mushroom, *Armillaria tabescens*, a species not found in Norway. Lincoff lived right next to Central Park and every morning during the season he would do a little recce of the park before work, noting how fresh growths were coming on and whether he needed to come back in one, two, or three days. Some mushrooms appear early in the season, others fruit later. Lincoff adjusted his purposeful rounds accordingly. In this way he could monitor his secret places in Central Park on a daily basis. And if he needed some mushrooms for dinner all he had to do was run across the street and pick up a tasty morsel or two. We walked on through the park, with Lincoff providing a running commentary on which mushrooms one could find by which trees and when in the season one might expect to find them.

We also found some other interesting edible plants, among them what Lincoff called Poor Man's Pepper, *Lepidium virginicum*, a plant with an upright stem and white flowers growing out from it, rather like a bottle brush. The whole of this plant, which is part of the mustard family, can be eaten: the seeds can be used in the same way as black pepper and the flowers and leaves can be sprinkled over a salad to give it a slightly peppery flavour.

We came round a bend and there was one of the park-keepers. He gave a little cough to attract our attention.

'Have you been picking mushrooms?' the elderly park-keeper asked.

In Norway, everyone has the right to pick berries, mushrooms, or flowers anywhere — not just in the countryside, but on private land too, if it's uncultivated. The same rule does not apply, however, to a park in the United States. We had been caught red-handed.

'What sort is that?' he asked amiably, pointing into Lincoff's basket.

Lincoff answered promptly, listing the species by their Latin names.

'It is my duty to inform you that it is forbidden to pick flowers or plants in Central Park. There, that's my job done!' he said, grinning as he sauntered off. A perfect example of sound bureaucratic common sense.

Anthropologists calculate that hunter-gatherer tribes do not need to work more than 17 hours a week in order to have enough to eat. For many people today, hunting and gathering are activities which satisfy a longing for the outdoor life and/or a desire to meet people, and not primarily a way of putting food on the table. But this does not mean that mushroom enthusiasts take the hunt any less seriously than the hunter-gatherer tribes of the world. An interest in mushrooms can awaken primeval foraging instincts you didn't know you had.

Lincoff told me that, since 2006, the New York Mycological Society has been running a registration project in Central Park. So far they have found 400 species of mushroom, including five species of chanterelle. This compares with the approximately 500 species of plants registered as growing in the park. It was in Central Park that I found the mushroom which the Chinese value above all others, due to its medicinal properties — *Ganoderma lucidum*, the Lingzhi Mushroom. The Ancient Chinese believed this mushroom could give a person immortality. In modern China it can be bought in the traditional medical halls and is used in the treatment of cancer, heart problems, and many other ailments. If only sick people in Chinatown, in Lower Manhattan, knew that all they had to do was take the subway to Central Park, instead of having to pay the prices charged by the Chinese herbalists. I laid the lingzhis gently in my basket. They would make a lovely present for my old mum in Malaysia. No one there sees anything contradictory in combining Western and Eastern medicine. Using all the means at your disposal when necessary is regarded more as a sensible insurance policy. I could just picture her serving lingzhi tea from New York's Central Park to her friends when it was her turn to play hostess.

My walk through Central Park with Gary Lincoff is a good example of what it is like to go mushroom hunting when you actually have a treasure map of the terrain.

I went mushroom hunting in Central Park with a man who enjoyed rock star status in American mycology circles. A new world was revealed to me. I should have been over the moon, but I wasn't. The truth was that I didn't feel a thing. If it were anatomically possible I would have said that my heart had been dislocated. Eiolf's sudden death had taken a physical, mental, and emotional toll on me. Every cell in my body was on red alert, running on adrenalin. Can feelings be paralysed by grief? Perhaps grief induces a sort of general anaesthesia? Perhaps that was why I was completely numb? It was almost as if I had lost touch with my emotions. I could find no words to describe how I felt, no words I could hold on to. In the eye of grief's tornado there are no words.

A wall had fallen away and I was alone and exposed, wide-open to wind and weather. Sorrow sucked all the life out of me. Despite the fact that I was surrounded by caring family and friends, the loneliness was absolute. I felt as though I was shrivelling up from the inside. All that was left was a paler, stupider, ashen version of myself. I began to wonder whether I needed new glasses and I had difficulty hearing what was said. My sense of smell more or less disappeared and food tasted like cardboard. It was almost as if my senses had been put out of action. I, who used to just close my eyes and go to sleep, now lay awake, counting the hours in the dark of night. At such times thoughts and images fought for space. My concentration was dimmed, at a low ebb, and I missed the old me. The newspapers and magazines we subscribed to piled up, unread.

More than once I found myself standing outside the front door not knowing which key to use. It took me ages to get any work done. Practical tasks became almost insurmountable. I had no idea what I did with the time. It simply ran between my fingers. Was this what it was like to be a time optimist and never be able to meet a deadline? For once I found myself sympathising with scatterbrains who were always slow and persistently late. I forgot appointments that I had noted in my diary. I ate next to nothing. People gave me books about mourning, but the words just danced about in front of my eyes, singly, not even in whole sentences. I, who had always been a bookworm, could remember nothing of whatever I tried to read. I, who loved music, found it impossible to play our favourite records. I got a huge lump in my throat at the mere sound of the first familiar stanzas. Grief calls for muscles for which no fitness centre has the right exercise machines.

On one occasion I plucked up my courage and went to a big party at a friend's house, but had to leave before the dancing began. It was all just too much. My friend was a tango fanatic and had booked a little introductory tango session for us. The old me would have loved to try that, but I was weary to the bone. The shock of Eiolf's death had plunged me into a deep well and apathy settled over me like a thick blanket that I couldn't kick off. Television discussions about politics and social issues seemed banal and devoid of sense or purpose. The debating rituals in which commentators played their respective parts in a well-known drama were nothing but wooden acting and mechanical mouthings to me. The petty details of everyday life seemed even more pointless. Nothing could interest or upset me. Life had been watered down. I felt a vague, nagging unease, although I didn't know how to describe it or stop it.

It was as if I was wearing an invisibility suit. The world went on without me.

'Where did you find that mushroom?'

Stories of amazing discoveries of capricious, unpredictable mushrooms in secret spots form a *leitmotif* in mushroom circles, repeated again and again. Sites are ranked as good safe bets or as undependable and even untrustworthy, but their addresses are and will remain secret. When out mushrooming, it can be hard to spot your quarry, even when it is right under your nose, because mushrooms can be very well hidden, camouflaged by leaves and grass, twigs and pine needles. For that very reason it helps to have precise coordinates for sites that could stand to be searched more thoroughly. Otherwise it's like looking for the proverbial needle in a haystack.

Secret mushrooming sites are not general or vague areas. They are often very precisely and specifically defined, right down to individual trees. If, for example, you are hunting for chanterelles it's no use looking under just any tree, deciduous or conifer, you have to look under the one tree which lives in symbiosis with the chanterelle mycelium. When rainfall, temperature, microclimatic conditions, and other key variables coincide in a very particular fashion this can result in a much sought after mushroom. Which is why mushroom gatherers weigh up various alternatives on Nature's intricate Rubik's cube before setting out on an expedition. There should not have been too much rain. Or too little. It should not be too hot. Or too cold. The length of time since regular haunts were last visited also has to be taken into account. Predicting when certain mushrooms will appear is not unlike an astrological reading. When the heavenly bodies are in perfect alignment wonderful things can happen. But there can be many barriers to overcome before you achieve that bingo moment of finding the prize you seek. Even in the most secret spots there is no guarantee that it will be there when you show up.

In this, mushroom hunters are like economists. Both parties can always explain (away) why an anticipated result was not achieved. The same applies to explanations for so-called good or bad mushroom years. There are always plenty of theories as to why a particular combination of early or late summer heat or rain ensured an excellent or a terrible season.

Whether it is a good mushroom year or not is, of course, something that can be determined with a degree of objectivity, but it is also a matter of attitude. Is your basket half-empty or half-full? Those who like a little grumble will always harp on about how poor the crop has been, no matter what.

Nevertheless, the more secret places you know of, the greater your chances of hitting the jackpot.

There is another, depressing, side to such knowledge, though, and that is the destruction of treasured locations due to rampant tree felling and bulldozing. At the start of each mushroom season pictures are posted on social media of trees cut down and lying scattered all over the place. Another prime hunting ground gone. It can be therapeutic to share one's disappointment with like-minded souls who understand what a loss this is. You can almost hear the whole community heave a great collective sigh.

Anyone who has been around mushroomers will have noticed how the experienced gatherer will bend down and pick a mushroom with tentative hand and rapt attention. Carefully he holds the mushroom up to the light and studies it. The mushroom is then turned gently upside down and the underside raised to the nose that is waiting, ready to carry out the vital smell test. He screws up his face, opening nostrils that almost quiver as he inhales the scent of the mushroom. If he is with other mushroomers and an unusual specimen is found it will be passed round so that everyone can examine it. This process is repeated with or without a magnifying glass while the mushroom is inspected, twisted and turned this way and that. This can take time. There will be some discussion back and forth before the person regarded as the sage of the group pronounces their answer. If, however, it is not possible to confirm the identity of the mushroom then and there, anyone wishing to pursue the matter will take the mushroom home with them to conduct an even more thorough examination, using a microscope and other aids. All part of a perfectly normal day in the woods for mushroom gatherers, though to the uninitiated it may seem like an arcane sectarian rite.

When told by a proud mushroom forager of some fabulous finds, it is not unusual to respond by asking where these mushrooms were discovered. Such a question can elicit a variety of reactions. Most mushroomers have learned how to answer politely without giving away a nanogram of relevant geographical information. But I have also seen people clam up so tight anyone would have thought I had been asking for their bank card pin code. I once asked someone I thought was a friend where he had found his mushrooms. Obviously I wasn't expecting to be given the exact coordinates for the place, but I did have some small hope of being provided with a little information as to the general location. Instead all I received was the useless and utterly worthless reply: 'Oslo.' That earned him a big, black mark in my book.

On another occasion, when I was out with a generous fellow mushroomer, he showed me his Penny Bun spot. The Penny Bun, *Boletus edulis,* also known widely as porcini or cep, is a much sought after mushroom. Some people consider it the king of edible mushrooms. The place my friend showed me lay in an area popular with Sunday walkers. My friend told me how he had once been faced with what could only be described as a serious mycological and moral dilemma. One day, some years earlier, he had come across some beautiful little Penny Buns which he decided to leave where they were, to allow them to grow a little more. He covered the mushrooms with some dry leaves, so they wouldn't be seen from the path: he is not alone in employing this tactic of covering very small mushrooms with organic matter of one sort and another from the forest, then returning a few days later. The keenest foragers have all found mushrooms which they have left alone, hoping to be able to pick them later, when they are a bit bigger. The trick with this is to get back to them before anyone else finds them. After a day or two my contact returned to his Penny Bun spot, full of anticipation. His heart sank when, while still some way off, he saw a man, a scruffy tramp, lying on his mushrooms. What a dreadful situation for an enthusiastic mushroom hunter. You might think it couldn't get any worse, but it did. Because the man was, in fact, stone dead. And he was lying *right on top of* the Penny Buns. What do you do? I'm glad to say my friend did not hesitate for a second. He did the only right thing, also from a mycological point of view. He called the police.

My friend and I found no Penny Buns that day, but I always think of that tramp when we go there to look for them.

Basically, one can simply assume that everyone keeps their favourite sites to themselves. So no one expects to be given GPS coordinates. Anyone asking questions will give up as soon as they detect the slightest sign of hesitation. Mushroomers can be pretty sensitive on that score. No Guantánamo interrogation methods here. When asked where a mushroom was found it is both normal and perfectly acceptable to reply in somewhat vague and elliptical terms, such as 'Solemskogen' (Solem Forest) or 'Østmarka' (Eastern Woodlands), and leave it at that. A polite little dance, a delicate *pas de deux*, is quite common when such questions come up. You weave in some information on general, mushroom related conditions such as rainfall and temperature and make a show of giving and taking without any real intelligence to speak of being exchanged. This way you are able to give an answer, and the person asking feels that she has learned something that might come in handy. An expert mushroom gatherer is also skilled in evasion tactics.

One day, a female mushroom buddy of mine let slip somewhat confidentially that she had visited a particular spot, a place known to both of us, looking for St George's mushrooms.

'Did you look under the larches?' I asked, because I knew that St George's mushrooms sometimes grew there.

'No, not there, somewhere else,' she said, and no more than that. I understood that she didn't want to say any more and that I shouldn't dig any deeper.

As a novice, you may well think yourself lucky when someone actually invites you to go mushrooming with them. But there is always a risk of being disappointed. An invitation to go mushroom hunting is not an invitation to share your host's secret places.

'Where should we go?' another female mushroom buddy asked me once, as we were entered an Oslo park.

It is quite possible to find good edible mushrooms on a stroll through the city, without having to clamber up steep slopes, crawl under toppled trees, or fight one's way over rapids or muddy streams. There are also plenty of tasty 'urban' mushrooms to be had. This particular park was a big one and divided into several geographically distinct areas. I knew that my companion had made a lot of interesting finds here, so my hopes were high. But she clearly had no intention of showing me where she had made her most exciting discoveries. Not that day, anyway. If she had been minded to do so she would have taken the lead, saying something like, 'Let's go this way.' We tramped around over by the fence on one side of the park and found nothing. A mite disappointed, we did a round of the other side, but had no luck there either. I showed her a place where I had frequently found St George's mushrooms, *Calocybe gambosa,* the first mushroom treat of the spring. Then my friend pointed to a spot where she usually found Scotch Bonnets, *Marasmius oreades,* a small and very tasty mushroom. In other words, we exchanged 'useless' information on mushrooms which were not in season, but wrapped up as little titbits shared only with a close friend. We don't usually carry a basket in the city, but we do always have some discreet equipment on us: a paper bag in the rucksack, a small knife. Neither of these was called for on this occasion and we eventually went our separate ways, empty-handed. There is a fine art to going mushroom hunting with a fellow enthusiast without revealing the secret of your own best spots.

If you don't know anyone willing to share their favourite mushroom sites with you, you can always try to glean what you can from the mass of information in the public domain. The website *artsobservasjoner.no* is an online information bank on the wealth of flora and fauna in Norway. It provides a continually updated register of species sightings, including mushrooms, throughout the country. Enter the name of the mushroom in which you are interested on the site's map and, if you are lucky, you will be supplied with the exact coordinates of earlier finds in your district — a service I have occasionally availed myself of, with good results. In other countries, websites like observation. org and inaturalist.org are also useful.

If you don't have any secret mushroom sites, social media is not a bad place to start either. I've picked up lots of tips on good locations from websites and blogs dedicated to mushroom enthusiasts. Most of the activity on these sites involves reports of large or unusual finds. At the start of the season the focus is on finding the first true morel, a great moment, one which can bring stars to the eyes. A report in June that 'chanterelles have been found in Sarpsborg' means that they are likely to appear in the Oslo area within a week or so. The mushroom gods willing. Towards the end of the year, it becomes something akin to a competition to announce the finding of the last Funnel chanterelle, *Craterellus tubaeformis*, an event which usually occurs around Christmas. Thus, social media acts as a barometer of sorts as well, monitoring the peaks and troughs of the season. Posts on social media can also provide inspiration for new mushroom hunting destinations to save simply functioning on autopilot; going back, in one's sleep almost, to well-trodden spots. And, by following international websites and blogs, you can extend the season virtually and indulge your passion for mushrooms all year round.

Some members of the mushroom community demonstrate their disapproval of the prevailing culture of secrecy by actively sharing their favourite sites as a matter of principle. With guides like these you are not being sent off on a treasure hunt with a half-finished map. If you start to plot in such tips systematically you can gradually build up an index of interesting foraging sites. It is important to point out, however, that such individuals can be counted on one hand. One who I found particularly interesting was R., due to her almost daily updates and excellent nature photography. Since then I have actually met her in person. She had offered to show me one of her special places in Oslo, which very few people knew about because it lay on a private island. A shared destiny as mycology nerds led to my being shown a secret mushroom patch by someone who I had previously only communicated with via social media. This was a novel experience for me.

It helps to know some good sites, but you can also increase your chances of striking lucky by familiarising yourself with the standard 'tree partners' of certain fungi. Many mushrooms enjoy a symbiotic relationship or so-called 'mycorrhiza' with certain species of tree. Once I discovered this, my knowledge of Norwegian trees underwent a steep learning curve. All green plants partake in so-called nutrient exchange partnerships, in which fungi supply over 80 per cent of a plant's nitrogen needs. It is no exaggeration, therefore, to say that this interaction forms the basis of all life on Earth. If you want to find chanterelles then it is best to search in pinewoods and not pastureland or meadows. In pastureland one is more likely to find other species.

The Penny Bun, which so many dream of, is found in pine, fir, birch, or oak forests. It is also worth knowing a bit about the age of the forest, the soil, and the topography. Some mushrooms get on so well together that if you find one there's a good chance you'll also find the other. So, for example, the Rosy Spike-Cap, *Gomphidius roseus*, and the Jersey Cow Mushroom, *Suillus bovinus*, are always close companions.

I learned that it is more or less an unwritten rule in mycology circles never to go back to another person's secret sites if you have been fortunate enough to be shown them. It can really rankle to discover that someone you trusted enough to show them your gathering grounds has started going there on their own, without explicitly having been given permission to do so. Mushroomers feel a strong sense of ownership towards such secret sites. So it can be very upsetting to discover that rascally outsiders have been picking mushrooms from 'your' patch. Like other gatherers in the forest, mushroomers feel that they have a legitimate claim to 'their' secret gathering spots. The possessive pronoun is used with the greatest matter-of-course: 'my cloudberry marsh', 'my chanterelle spot' and so on. This tendency is not a problem as long as you don't run into someone who feels equally entitled to pick from the *same* spot. In order to defuse a potentially tense situation you may have to feel your way to an unspoken agreement with your rival, to establish the boundaries for who picks where. If, that is, the whole thing cannot be sorted out with a quiet little chat. The problem arises when the two parties involved do not agree on the tacit rules regarding right of ownership, among them how to resolve such stand-offs in the forest. I have never heard of anyone actually resorting to physical violence, but such situations can give rise to a lot of sighing, moaning, and annoyance. And, not least, sadness because one's secret place is a secret no more.

Slowly but surely, as time went on, the pattern of my days began to change. It was when I was free to go mushroom hunting that this new life gradually began to blossom. These outings gave me the push I needed to get out of the house and take part in life, instead of staying immersed in misery within its four walls. It also made it easier to get to know people in the mushroom community, who made me feel welcome on their outings. I was taken to places in and around Oslo which were totally unknown to me.

On these forays into moss-covered forests I also began to take pleasure in gathering other wild delicacies: wood club-rushes, ostrich ferns, and livelong, spruce tips, rosebay willowherb, and wood sorrel. Plants that I had once regarded simply as general woodland greenery or weeds at the side of the road now provided the inspiration for novel culinary experiences with a new circle of friends. With each new mushroom I learned to identify, every new site I visited, and every new mushroom buddy I made, I gradually became more integrated into the community. And, although I didn't know it, each of these experiences represented another tiny mouse-step towards the end of the black tunnel of mourning.

No wonder people talk about a vacuum after someone dies. There are so many hours in the day that have to be filled when someone very close to us passes away. For me, these forays into the fungi kingdom became a way of spending this unwonted spare time. And as I became more familiar with certain forests I also ventured to go out hunting on my own, with only my mushroom basket and newly acquired knowledge for company. Visiting my favourite spots was rather like coming home. I knew exactly where to go, I didn't simply wander around aimlessly as I had when I was an absolute beginner. It was almost as if I had a checklist of particular places in each forest that I ought to cast a more careful eye over. Those woodland walks brought me inner peace. The outdoor type? *Moi?* And did I also become a little more Norwegian? I'm not sure, but whatever the case, it was both fresh and liberating.

The dream

I dreamed of becoming part of the inner circle of the mushroom community: the mushroom inspectors who conduct checks on mushrooms picked in the wild throughout the season. I was impressed by the extent of their knowledge and the sense of 'vocation' that prompted them to spend their free time helping residents of Oslo who wished to pick mushrooms. For the first time since Eiolf's death I felt that I had a goal and a direction.

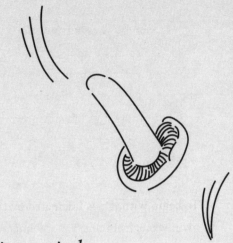

The inner circle

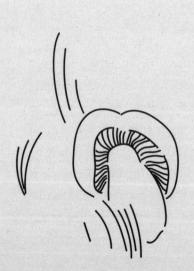

To begin with, I was fascinated by the apparent classlessness of my mycological society. Only much later did I realise that here too there was, in fact, an invisible hierarchy. In an organisation which sets great store by learning, a pecking order quite naturally develops, according to levels of expertise. Although this is not an exact science, everyone seems to know who to ask when it comes to identifying an unknown mushroom. The mysterious fungus will always land in the lap of whoever is regarded as the most knowledgeable and competent.

From the outside, the mushrooming community may seem rather like a cult dedicated to the knowledge of mushrooms, in which expertise confers social prestige. Due to new advances in the scientific world, the boundaries of knowledge are constantly expanding. What was thought to be true last year may not be the case today, so knowledgeable experts are both respected and valued. At the very top of the pyramid are the mycologists, who have their university diplomas as proof that they know their stuff. As someone new to the game, I did not immediately discern the demarcation line between mycologists and the group below them — the certified mushroom professionals. Many certified professionals are both extremely knowledgeable and highly experienced. Within this group, individuals are ranked according to seniority. Here, it is not one's biological age that matters, but which year one sat the inspector's exam. That, and how active one is as a mushroom inspector. It is among these senior authorities one finds the inner circle from which come most of the society's office bearers.

In a class of their own are the select few who have had a species of mushroom named after them. Their number can be counted on one hand. It is interesting to note that it is not only mycologists who belong to this exclusive club. Some species of mushrooms have been called after amateurs or spouses.

People who are interested in gathering mushrooms, but who lack the basic know-how — weekend mushroomers — are the focus of much of the local societies' educational and outreach work. Some are bitten by the bug and sign up for the organised courses and expeditions. Others are of a mindset that can easily turn a hobby into a high-risk sport. They think they know enough and don't bother getting their mushrooms checked. They should, however, perhaps consider doing so. Statistics from the Norwegian Mycological Association show that, in 2016, toxic mushrooms were found in 10 per cent of all baskets checked. A total of 86 deadly poisonous specimens were found in these baskets.

The simplest way of finding out which unofficial sub-category a mushroom gatherer belongs to is to ask what they have in their basket. And all will be revealed.

One short cut to mushroom credibility is to find a rare mushroom. This is partly because seasoned foragers are, for the most part, really no different from any other nerds. Just as mountaineers rank peaks according to how hard they are to climb and birdwatchers set the greatest store by those birds that are the most difficult to spot, so the most exciting thing for mycology nerds is to discover mushrooms they have never come across before, species that are rare and hence extremely hard to find, or that may even be 'red-listed', which is to say species that are in danger of dying out. Finding the first true morel or Penny Bun of the season also gives one a certain 'mushroom cred', but this doesn't last long. Luck doesn't count for much in a cult dedicated to knowledge. The year's first or biggest chanterelle is only a big sensation on social media, and a short-lived one at that.

The real heroes of the association are the people who spend so much of their spare time painstakingly logging their finds on a national database. These entries provide a picture of the distribution of different species, the environments in which they thrive, and how these have changed over time. This knowledge is vital to the management of the countryside. The work of recording mushroom finds is, therefore, very important. Every year the Norwegian Mycological Association presents an award to the person who has logged the most finds in that year. Now and again one reads in the tabloids of a rare mushroom putting a stop to the extension of a motorway or some other building project. Often, in such cases, it is databases like this that are responsible.

Amanita muscania, Fly Agaric

Mushroom friendships

Secret places play an important part in mushroom friendships. Mushroom sites are especially nice presents for good mushroom friends to give, share, and exchange. They remind me of the Japanese cards we used to collect in Malaysia when I was a child. Some kids always had more of the really brilliant cards, the ones that everyone wanted. There was a brisk trade in the cards at break, with lots of hard bargaining. The gift of a great card was a sure sign of eternal friendship. Similarly, secret mushroom spots are a hard currency within the mushrooming community, and to be shown someone's secret place is a great vote of confidence.

I was happy, therefore, when a new mushroom buddy offered to show me a place where the Yellow Foot Mushroom, *Craterellus lutescens*, grew. This was the first time anyone had volunteered to show me their special site and I was very touched. Sharing a secret site forges even closer bonds of friendship. Suddenly we went from being mere acquaintances to being good mushroom friends. Marcel Mauss' little book *The Gift* is a classic sociological work. It spotlights the way in which the exchange of gifts between groups influences the relationships within them. People who enjoy good relationships with each other exchange gifts, and these gifts foster even better relationships because they bind the giver and the receiver together, in a sort of chicken and egg logic. According to Mauss, it is important to give, to receive, and, not least, to reciprocate. This reciprocation is the glue that holds the relationship together. Everyone who gives and receives Christmas presents understands this principle.

I remember when one of my new friends offered to show me their St George's mushroom spot. That first year we found only three. And there were three of us, so that meant one each. The St George's mushroom is the fanfare that heralds the start of the mushroom season. When the snow is gone and the days begin to get longer and lighter, it's good to dust off your mushroom basket and go out hunting at a time when there are few other mushrooms around. For this very reason, my local mycological society organises its own annual St George's trip. Usually to the island of Hovedøya in Oslo Fjord or Kongeskogen forest on the peninsula of Bygdøy. It is hard to say exactly when the mushroom will appear, as organisers of the St George's trips have learned the hard way year after year. According to veteran members of the society, in the old days this mushroom was never seen in the Oslo area before the end of May, and often not until well into June. However, due in part to climate change perhaps, the start of the mushroom season has shifted and is now earlier. It is not inconceivable, therefore, that in Norway in the future we'll be able to find St George's mushrooms on St George's day itself, 23 April. *Calocybe gambosa* derives its common name from the fact that in the British Isles it can appear as early as the English patron saint's day. The St George's mushroom is squat and meaty, with a creamy white cap, gills, and stem. Many people believe that this mushroom has a strong, mealy scent, like wet flour, others maintain that it smells more like waffle batter, which only goes to show how hard it can be to describe or find a good simile for a particular odour. The St George's mushroom grows in the chalky soil around Oslo Fjord, but since it can be confused with certain poisonous fungi it is not a species for beginners. An interesting feature of spring mushrooms is that many of them are decomposers, which is to say they grow on substrates such as pine cones, twigs, and branches lying deep underground. The St George's grows in grassy fields and pasture land, but it can also be found in deciduous forests and hedgerows. It is not uncommon to find fairy rings or large colonies of St George's mushrooms. They tend to come up in the same spot year after year, so if you know of a St George's spot then you can be pretty sure of a good start to the season. I was delighted, therefore, by this offer to share a St George's site.

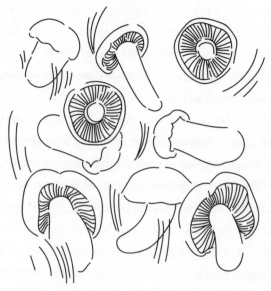

Calocybe gambosa, St George's mushrooms

Practical knowledge is the key to passing the mushroom inspector's exam, but when I first joined my local society I didn't have anyone to go foraging with. I knew that if I was to pass the exam I would have to go out with experienced mushroomers as often as I could.

I decided therefore to hold a mushroom themed dinner at my home and ask everyone who came to bring a dish made with mushrooms. I posted the invitation on the society's Facebook page and a few adventurous souls took me up on it. A quick round of introductions revealed us to be a pretty diverse bunch. There was plenty of good food: smoked reindeer hearts with white truffle caviar, mushroom pie, mushroom bread, mushroom pâté with sherry and miso, Penny Bun ravioli in Penny Bun sauce, reindeer carpaccio in Funnel chanterelle sauce, Portobellos stuffed with *chèvre*, green salad with chanterelle vinaigrette, blue cheese with Funnel chanterelle marmalade, and finally, almond sponge cake with a croquant mushroom topping.

When the keenest mushroom hunters are gathered together on a cold day in February, with the snow falling in big wet flakes outside, the conversation quite naturally turns to their shared passion. They are restless; they talk about mushrooms they have picked and mushrooms they're planning to pick. The desire for the season to start soon is acute. It is a yearning that lies deep and pushes up to the surface when it has been far too long since the last trip to the forest. You can hear it in their voices and the way they talk. It is a need, a craving for fungi, of which true mushroomers can never be free. Such individuals cannot wait for the happy days they know are coming, and for the most dedicated the season starts as early as the middle of May. For the more senior members of the association, this is a hobby with an in-built health insurance. Their longing for mushrooms draws even the frailest of them out into the woods, makes them quicken their step when they see something interesting farther on and bend down and stretch old muscles when there's a mushroom to pick. Mushrooms are food for both body and soul. This is a group who will happily extend the season, with headlamps, warm winter clothing, and plenty of vim and vigour, looking for the year's last Funnel chanterelle among the patches of snow. I've picked Funnel chanterelles on 23 December myself.

Many of my best mushroom friends today attended the mushroom dinner I arranged the winter before I took the inspector's exam.

One of my new mushroom buddies once took me and another mushrooming novice to a park where we found some mushrooms from the *Agaricus* genus. I was thrilled with my haul and felt deliriously well-off. I had long wished to learn more about *Agaricus* mushrooms and we found several species, both edible and inedible. Even though the Prince wasn't among the edible ones we found, I was very happy. The following year, my friend and I went back to that same place, and this time he showed me *another* spot where he *always* found Prince mushrooms. Since it was rather early in the season and the ground was a bit dry, he asked me to help him water the places where they usually came up. He showed me where the watering cans hung and how to go back and forth over the ground, giving it a good soaking. It was clearly not the first time he had watered Prince mushrooms there. This little episode taught me that the sharing of secret mushroom grounds can be done in stages. Even when you have been shown one secret site, you may still not have been introduced to the real prime patch. It was always possible that my friend knew of an even better spot in that same area, and if we remained friends he might share it with me some day.

I would later discover that my friend's habit of watering mushrooms was a long-standing one. It's one thing to know where to pick some tasty titbits, quite another to speed those goodies along. Once, many years ago, this same friend had been very keen to show a young woman some St George's mushrooms, which she had never picked before. So he was over the moon when he found a few tiny specimens in the forest — but there had been no rain for some time, would they be big enough by the weekend, in time for his lady friend's visit? He couldn't rely on the meteorologists or the weather, so my friend simply took matters into his own hands. He loaded up his car with buckets of water and drove out to the forest to water the St George's mushrooms himself, to ensure that they would nice and big for his friend's visit. This story had a very happy ending: the watering of those mushrooms led to wedding bells.

After I had been part of the mushroom community for a while, I began to see that the most seasoned mushroomers have a map in their head on which details of each find — species, time, and place — are precisely plotted. Some people can be extremely specific in their descriptions, saying things like: 'I found that mushroom in 1986, it was growing between X and Y.' This information is usually presented with the greatest certainty. One of the main conclusions from research into memory is, however, that it is unreliable and easily influenced, and can often play tricks on us. We tend to grin superciliously at hunters and fishermen who are clearly inflating the size of the day's catch. Can we be sure that the mushroom hunter isn't suffering from the same exaggeration syndrome? Might memories of our own best discoveries be equally unreliable? The Penny Bun you once found may have been big and beautiful, but how accurate is your recollection of the particulars: year, location, and so on. Why are some veteran mushroomers so sure their memories serve them right?

Agaricus augustus, Prince mushrooms

One day while out foraging, I stumbled on what I think may be the answer. There was one particular species of mushroom that I'd been after for some time, but had never found. On that particular day, the hairs on my arm stood on end as it dawned on me that it might be within reach. I knew straight away what I had found. My status in the mycological knowledge cult went up a notch. It was an almost spiritual experience. That was the day when I found Prince mushrooms, *Agaricus augustus*, for the first time. I was alone and almost panicked slightly. How could I get my find confirmed as quickly as possible? There were so many of them, both large and small, that I almost forgot to breathe. This discovery seemed totally undeserved, like being allowed to lap up the vanilla custard filling without having to eat the rest of the bun first. I had never seen a Prince mushroom in real life before, but it is quite a distinctive mushroom, so I was pretty sure I was right.

The Prince mushroom can grow quite large, reaching as much as 22 centimetres in diameter. And it can be relatively heavy. The biggest one I have found weighed 300 grams. It has a scaly brown cap and a white stem. If you cut into the stem, the inside feels both firm and silky smooth. How strange to think of it growing right alongside what for years had been my regular route to and from work. It had been there all the time, so near and yet so far, before I even knew of its existence. The Prince mushroom is seldom attacked by maggots. To me, its most distinctive feature is its scent. It has a delicious smell of almonds. And if you don't know how almonds smell, just take a sniff of Amaretto liqueur, made from a base of almonds and apricot stones. I still remember so well the heady thrill of finding my first Prince mushrooms in a spot I had come upon by pure chance, a wonderful and unexpected moment that activated the memory sensors and branded the details on my mind: the trees round about, the angle of the slope, how the sun fell through the branches, and so on. I had just said goodbye to two mushroom friends. We had been unsuccessful in our hunt and we had decided to call it a day. I was on my way home when I decided to take a short cut. It was rather shady in the short passage, with tall trees on one side and some low bushes on the other. Only pedestrians and cyclists used the narrow passageway. Suddenly my eye caught the mushrooms on the slope beneath the tall trees. I scrambled up to take a closer look. I scratched the stem of the mushroom and the smell of almonds flooded me. I knew immediately this was a special find.

Scientists refer to such highly detailed recollections as *flash-bulb memories*. Memories are often evoked by some dramatic and emotive event. So, for older generations the question, 'Where were you when you heard President Kennedy had been assassinated?' will elicit total, vivid recall of that moment. Some scientists believe that these flashbulb memories are completely infallible because they are based on factors, primarily emotional in nature, that hold some significance for a person. Is it this flashbulb mechanism which enables mushroomers to remember their most spectacular discoveries in perfect 3D? Whatever the case, it may well have been the discovery of my own first secret spot for a prize mushroom — the Prince of mushrooms itself — that sealed my fate as a mushroom addict.

How awful then to promptly be robbed of my secret. I had only ever shown my Prince mushroom spot to two people. One of these was a trusty mushroom friend who had shared many of his most closely guarded sites with me. It was good to be able to return the favour and redress the balance slightly: till then the sharing had gone only one way and all to my advantage. The other was my good friend J., who had no special interest in mushrooms, but who had been kind enough to act as driver when I needed help to transport my Prince mushrooms — I found so many on that first occasion that public transport was not an option. Sadly, just afterwards he revealed my secret, quite casually, to someone he happened to fall into conversation with. I couldn't believe my ears when I heard. I almost wept, it was such bad news. I couldn't understand how anyone could be so thoughtless. Although J. may not have appreciated the gravity of what he had done. That place meant nothing to him, but it was worth its weight in gold to me. It was, after all, the one place that had been exclusively mine. But even as I was fuming over this 'betrayal', I was also observing myself and noting how quickly I had become a true mushroomer. I had, of course, heard of all the secrecy in the mushrooming community, but hadn't given it much thought. That was before I had a secret spot of my own, though. It's rather like the boiling frog experiment, in which the frog doesn't realise the water is getting hotter until it's too late. Was I becoming as obsessed with mushrooms as the people I was now mixing with? Had I become an unbearable nerd? Had I turned into a mad mushroomer, so gradually that I hadn't even noticed?

The first person to detect mycomania, or mushroom madness, is usually an individual's other half. Some mushroom widows and widowers have been known to present their mad mushroomer with an impossible ultimatum: it's either them or the fungi. As far as these spouses are concerned, mushroom gathering takes up too much time, money, and cupboard space. Other spouses respond with goodwill and encouragement. Their partner's interest in mushrooms is not merely tolerated, it is also respected. Like the support network for an Olympic athlete, these family members are always ready to help. They drive their mad mushroomer out and pick them up, clean and eat the spoils, accompany them on mushrooming expeditions to other parts of the world, and happily take part in the 'spouses' programmes'. They are given to wearing caps, badges, and T-shirts from international mushroom festivals, the sort of thing mycomaniacs love to sport. A few even end up taking the inspector's exam themselves.

I was introduced to most of the sites I have logged on my mental database by one of the Norwegian Mycological Association's senior members, who is well-acquainted with a host of places in the Oslo area, a man who thinks nothing of driving a few extra miles to check the conditions at one particular site. And while we're there we might as well see how things are looking at another spot not far away. Thus a 'little' mushrooming trip can easily turn into a much longer expedition. This particular friend always has several baskets and other foraging equipment in his car, just in case.

After many an outing together, we have come up with an efficient division of labour. He drives slowly; I keep a look-out. If I catch sight of something that looks promising, I ask him to stop — what you might call drive-by mushrooming. It's then my job to hop out and check whether there really is anything worth stopping for. It's also my job to pick the 'less mycologically interesting' mushrooms. This usually means common edible mushrooms such as chanterelles and the like. My mushroom buddy's back has grown stiffer with age, so he always takes time to size up a mushroom and decide whether it's worth the effort to bend down, first to photograph it and then to pick it. Although he would much prefer it to be the other way round and for the mushroom to come to him. I always know when we've found something interesting because he starts to hum softly and contentedly.

This friend has one special place he has often told me about, a spot which was shown to him by a late mushroom buddy. One day, after numerous trips together, he suggested that we go for a drive — he had a particular place he wanted to show me, he said. I didn't think too much about it, but when we got there my friend said, 'You mustn't show this place to anyone.' He had never said that before, not of any of the countless sites to which he had introduced me in the past. I knew then that I was there, on that legendary spot, and I felt both honoured and very lucky.

The inspector's exam: the mushroomer's rite of passage

There has been a training course for mushroom inspectors in Norway since 1952. Aspiring inspectors are recommended not to sit the exam until a year after completing the training course, to ensure that the knowledge has really been absorbed and not merely acquired through hard swotting. Successful candidates can then assist at their local society's mushroom inspections, supervised by a more experienced inspector. This system is quite unique, there is nothing like it anywhere else in the world, both in terms of the training programme and the inspections. My respect for mushroom inspectors, who take responsibility for people's lives and health, rose considerably when I heard about this certification system.

Neither of the other Scandinavian countries, Sweden and Denmark, has anything like the Norwegian system. In Norway, mushroom inspection is so well-established that public bodies direct people to the Norwegian Mycological Association's inspection service on their websites. Outside of Scandinavia, the attitude is even more *laissez-faire*. In France it used to be possible to take one's mushrooms to the chemist's, because the identification and uses of mushrooms and other fungi was part of a pharmacist's education. Sadly this is no longer the case. Nowadays, when Frenchmen take their finds to the chemist they are advised to throw them all away. At a Mediterranean mycology and mushroom festival which I attended, the Frenchmen I spoke to were very interested to hear about the Norwegian mushroom inspector's exam. Many people envy this model, with its organised courses and official examination.

I remember the moment when I walked into the examination room. Along one wall was a long sideboard, and set out on this, on a row of paper plates, were the test mushrooms that awaited me. These I would have to identify one after another, in the order determined by the examiner. This is, first and foremost, a practical exam. Usually there will be one species to a plate, but sometimes two similar species will be mixed up on the same plate: false and real chanterelles, or Jelly Babies and Funnel chanterelles, for example. The examination board is at pains to point out that this is not because they want to set traps for the examinees, but simply because they wish to see how they react in a real-life situation, of the sort that can crop up during an inspection.

I sat at the end of a long table in the middle of the room. Way down at the far end of the room sat the administrative director of the Association, who was acting as observer. The censor sat halfway between us, stony-faced, saying not a word. The examiner was the only one to move, shuttling briskly between the sideboard and me, furnishing me with a steady stream of test mushrooms. Everyone was very focused. The exam was conducted swiftly. There was absolutely no time for small talk. Although I had been introduced to all three of them beforehand, their body language underlined the formality, not to say solemnity, of the situation.

It seemed to be over in no time. I recognised all of the mushrooms 'served' to me, but took time to examine each one anyway, turning them this way and that and sniffing them as I had been taught. After a short wait in the corridor, I was called in and informed of the result. I had passed. I was a certified mushroom inspector! There were smiles all round, we all shook hands very formally, and then I was presented with my diploma. I may even have curtsied as it was handed to me, I was so thrilled to have completed this rite of passage, which I had been hearing about ever since I joined that mushrooms for beginners course.

Back then, the thought of being able to identify 150 species of mushroom had seemed like a distant dream, but now I too was a member of the inner circle.

I think Eiolf would have been proud of me.

Now, with my inspector's badge hanging round my neck, I too could check mushrooms for those who were less sure of what they had found. I could actually help to save lives! Now I could also attend the local society's kick-off meeting at the start of the season and the summing up meeting at the end, along with the other members of the inner circle. At the summing-up meeting, the year's successful candidates, who had passed through the eye of the needle to become mushroom inspectors, are presented. Normally, at these meetings, there will also be a talk of the sort which only mushroom nerds can appreciate. An expert talks at length about their 30 year hunt for the tiny bonnet mushrooms that can be less than a millimetre in diameter. Names such as Saffrondrop Bonnet, Scarlet Bonnet, Pink Bonnet, and Burgundydrop Bonnet raise the whole talk onto a more lyrical plane. I feel almost like part of an art installation.

One of my female mushroom friends wasn't happy about me sitting the exam as soon as I did. Her point was that mushrooming is a slow, gradually maturing science. This may be why most potential candidates are under the impression that they have to wait a whole year after completing the inspector's course before they can sit the exam. I thought that too, but later I discovered that anyone can apply to sit the exam at any time. You don't even have to take the 40 hour inspector's course. Might this false rumour have been spread by those anxious to stress that knowledge of mushrooms needs time to grow and ripen? The fact that I passed the exam did nothing to alter my friend's opinion. When I told her I'd passed she still said I should have waited.

The relentless grieving process

According to national records, I was now neither married nor unmarried, but fell instead into another category: that of widow/widower. Although our status may not be readily apparent to society at large, those of us who belong to this discreet club can nod in recognition to our fellows, much as the members of a secret brotherhood — the owners of the same make of car, say — acknowledge one another.

I dutifully attended the meetings of the bereavement support group run by the Fransiskushjelpen, a Catholic charity organisation, which had been warmly recommended to me. I looked at all the so-called 'younger bereaved' in my group. Most of them were women who had lost their partners around the same time as myself. Some of them had been newly married, others had been in long-term relationships. Some had young children to see to. The occasional couple of hours they spent with the support group was the only time when they could give themselves up to their grief. Some had sympathetic employers, others did not. A few poor souls were not only mourning, but also having problems with other family members.

The first meeting I attended was not a cheery gathering. This was the first day at the school for widows. I wasn't sure if it was the right thing for me, but as long as I couldn't speak about Eiolf without crying I reckoned that I still needed support. The slightest thing, the slightest thought, could turn on the waterworks I hadn't known I had inside me, and since this organisation had a great deal of experience of bereavement counselling, I decided to follow the programme and not ask too many questions.

One advantage of the group was that here I could be myself. I didn't have to put on any sort of a front. Another effect of the support group was that I was able to see my own suffering in relief. It was an open group, which meant that now and again a new member would join us. It was always painful to listen to other people who had recently lost a loved one speak about their bereavement. I remember one woman, in particular, who kept her eyes fixed on the floor and found it impossible to speak. But even though she could hardly get a word out, everyone felt for her. I, for one, was instantly transported back to the welter of emotions that had overwhelmed me when Eiolf died. At the same time, though, I gradually began to see how far I had come in the tough process of grieving. I could look back at the distance I had covered, but I could also see the road ahead of me. For most people, this is possibly the greatest benefit to be had from such a support group.

Bereavement is an ice-cold concrete wall. Every bone in the body aches from being hurled against it. Everyone in the group spoke of frequent visits to the doctor. It is a fact that the immune system is weakened by grief. We were all suffering from monkey mind, with restless thoughts swinging and leaping all over the place. A few had tried meditation. Others had visited spas or gone on holidays. We were all in despair, expending a lot of energy and other resources in trying to find ways of remedying our loss. But what one simply has to accept is that there is no magic spell to conjure up a new life.

Can one choose not to grieve? Can one simply choose to be happy and grief free?

One thing I'm sure of: the mourning process does not follow a linear step-by-step pattern. It is complex and full of moveable parts. There is no straight, predictable arrow pointing upwards from a grief-stricken existence to a grief-free state. The way twists and turns, and so-called progress occurs when it suits the grief, not you. What was clear was that we had all been equally unprepared. Death had struck everyone in the support group with unexpected force, whether it had been on the cards or not.

'If there's anything I can do for you just call,' people said.

The problem was that I didn't know what I needed. Obviously there is no standard formula for how to be a good support to someone in mourning, but for me the map of my friends and acquaintances was redrawn after Eiolf's death. People whom I had thought would be right there by my side, solid as rocks, never showed their faces, while others who had previously been more peripheral friends provided tireless and thoughtful help. They didn't give up, but followed me at the pace of my grief. It warmed my heart, if only fleetingly. U., a faithful and inventive friend, responded by calling in sometimes after work — entirely off his own bat — with all the ingredients for a meal in his shopping bag. I would sit at the kitchen table and watch while he made dinner. The grieving also need to eat.

'How are you?' people would ask.

Three little words, a gentle overture to a conversation about nothing in particular or the one thing uppermost in my mind. I later came to see that what I, like so many others, needed most of all was for my loss to be acknowledged. Any avoidance of the subject had the exact opposite effect. There was little comfort to be had from people who chatted away about this, that, and the other, anything in fact but Eiolf. I regarded this blindness to what I really needed right then as an insult to my pain. I didn't need words of wisdom. I simply needed my position to be recognised. What I definitely did not need was to have to hide how I was feeling. I realise that some people are so afraid of death themselves that they find it impossible to do anything but pussyfoot around the issue, but I found it hard to accept that their fear was worse than the grief I felt. People in mourning need help to get things done and to ease the pain. A few gifted props and mainstays manage to do both. In my case, only a handful of people seemed able to gauge what stage I had reached in the grieving process. So it was good to be with a group of other, equally grief-stricken, individuals.

The lack of empathy and understanding shown by those around us was a recurring topic of conversation within the group. Was it my imagination or did friends and acquaintances avoid me like the plague? Was that because they didn't know what to say to me? Were they afraid of death, or was it the grief they found hard to deal with? If they didn't pick up the thread when I mentioned Eiolf it felt like betrayal and cowardice on their part, a betrayal of Eiolf's short life and cowardice in refusing to recognise my anguish. It was also a denial of the couple we had once been. We were silently erased.

That first year, I went along to the Franciskushjelpens All Souls' Day service. I was surprised to see that there were so many of us, and that we were all so very different in terms of age, sex, and other outward features. Had I met any of these people on the street I would never have known that they were grief-stricken; all of these people who had lost an anchor and been left to drift out into the world alone. When heavy sadness is hidden it also becomes private — and lonely. The All Souls' service was simple and striking. When we started, the hall was in total darkness, but as each of us lit a candle for the loved one we had lost, the room was filled with a wonderful light. A light that not only reached into every nook and cranny of the room, it also lifted our hearts. But still, when I left the service I couldn't help thinking of the weight of sorrow in that hall, and how invisible it was to the world around us.

This contrasts sharply with the approach taken in Malaysia, where there are so many rituals associated with death. These include the Malaysian Chinese custom of marking, for seven weeks, every seventh day after a person's death. Then the hundredth day and then the actual anniversary of their passing.

I opted for a 'light' version of this and commemorated the hundredth day, with the burial of Eiolf's ashes, and then the anniversary of his death. I was amazed, and comforted, to see how many people attended the memorial service for that first anniversary. I assumed that they weren't there for my sake, but that they were all still mourning, each in their own way, for Eiolf. I've noticed that where once there was silence, social media now provides a platform for such memorials. It's good to know that the world can change.

Widow with a small 'w'

After a number of people had taken me mushroom picking and shown me their special sites, I felt it was time to invite my new friends to dinner. As we sat there round the table it struck me that Eiolf didn't know any of my new mushroom acquaintances. To these new dinner-party friends I wasn't a widow with a large 'W' — as I was to our old mutual friends.

It was an odd thought for me, used as I had been, all my adult life, to having Eiolf as witness to my life. Eiolf was the one person whom I never needed to explain things to, things that meant something to just us two and held no significance for anyone else. When you lose the witness to your life you also lose a part of yourself.

At that moment I realised that a new chapter of my life was starting to take shape.

*Mushroom
misgivings*

I met Eiolf when I was an exchange student in Stavanger, a month after I arrived there from Malaysia. It was at a party held by a neighbour. He was a nice, friendly young man with rather long, thick, fair hair. He was also the first Norwegian I had met who knew where Malaysia was without having to look it up. He was curious and asked interesting questions. We talked all evening. And that conversation lasted all through our life together. I used to go to the library on my way home from school and sometimes I would run into him there. So I began to go to the library more often. And so did he. That was how it began, among the bookshelves — like any romantic comedy. I was so young. What did I know about choosing a partner for life? My father always said I won the jackpot in the lottery for good husbands.

Mushrooms never crossed the threshold of Eiolf's family home, not the shop-bought variety and certainly not wild mushrooms. Frozen pizza — the latest thing from abroad, which had just appeared in Norwegian supermarkets — never figured on the menu in his parents' home either, not because it was considered unhealthy to eat manufactured, ready-made meals, but probably because it was new and foreign. And I don't think the mushrooms on those pizzas made them any more appealing to my parents-in-law.

While many people find their way into the realm of fungi through searching for new delicacies for the dinner table, just as many will turn up their noses at the very word 'mushroom'. These two diametrically opposed viewpoints reflect a polarity that appears to have prevailed in Norway for a very long time.

Almost by chance, I came across an archive compiled by Norwegian Ethnological Research (NEG), which is based at the Norwegian Museum of Cultural History on the Bygdøy peninsula. NEG, founded in 1946, is a cultural archives institution which has collected over 40,000 personal accounts on all the different aspects of daily life in Norway. In 1997, NEG sent out a questionnaire entitled 'Mushrooms and berries'. They received 198 replies. The four-page questionnaire starts with a brief introduction, in which it says:

> We are interested in knowing what is being gathered
> in forests and fields, whether this springs from
> tradition or impulse, and what part the social
> aspect plays in these trips. How you preserve the
> various types of wild plants and how they are

used in the home is also of interest. Recipes will, therefore, be very gratefully received. In the case of all these aspects: what you gather, how you preserve it, and how you use the different sorts of berry and mushroom, things may have changed during the course of your own lifetime. We are more interested in your own personal experience than in more general views. Stories of specific occurrences and experiences relating to points covered in this questionnaire would be greatly welcomed.

I called NEG and arranged to visit them to go through the archive. I arrived at the agreed time to find that spring had finally come to the Norwegian Museum of Cultural History. The birds were vying for who could chirp out loudest the message that the bright days were here. I went through the Folk Museum's staff entrance into a building with thick, stone walls and was directed up the stairs and into a library with windows running all the way down one side. I had the place to myself. On a solitary desk sat a tall stack of folders, each one full of handwritten replies to the questionnaire. I would be the only person working there that day. My contact at NEG had told me that only one other person had ever shown any interest in the questionnaire on mushrooms and berries. It was strange to think that these replies had lain in the archive for decades until the day when I came to Bygdøy. I felt privileged and couldn't wait to see what I would find.

What was clear from the survey was that, while the majority of the respondents were in the habit of picking and eating berries, only a few had picked mushrooms. But the replies from those who neither picked nor ate the latter are also interesting, because they say something about attitudes. Mushrooms were not considered fit for human consumption then; they were, quite simply, an inferior sort of food. Several people wrote of how mushrooms were regarded as animal fodder. That this attitude prevailed even during the war years, when food was in short supply, says a lot. 'Better to have potatoes on their own than eat cattle fodder', as one respondent wrote.[2] And a woman from the Oppland area wrote, 'I remember my mother telling me about when she was a girl, working as a dairymaid. One evening when she went out to milk the cows they were gone ... and gone they stayed. So she headed over to V., about five miles one way. And there she found the cows, they had found some mushrooms which they were particularly fond of.'[3] Thanks to those mushrooms, this lady's mother did not get home till very late that night. In other words, the present-day antipathy to wild mushrooms goes back a long way. For children, then as now, mushrooms were something they could only look at, not touch, and certainly not eat — although it was all right to stamp on them for a bit of simple fun.

Mushrooms were so seldom seen on a dinner table then that a number of contributors described the first time they had eaten them. A woman from Østfold wrote: 'I knew an old lady who lived near us ... She picked chanterelles and puffballs. She would take me with her and then we would go back to her house and fry them up. That was when I learned to recognise those two mushrooms, and since then I've picked chanterelles myself, although my parents were wary of the whole mushroom thing.'[4] While a few of those who dared to taste mushrooms were positively surprised ('very pleasant'), others felt that they 'smelled funny' or were 'disgusting'.

Despite such misgivings, a number of people reported having occasionally eaten mushrooms as adults; saying, for example, 'mushrooms are the sort of thing people eat in hotels'. They were associated with high days and holidays, with special occasions. One person wrote, 'we used to buy mushrooms when we wanted to give ourselves a treat'. Tinned mushrooms, which could be bought in two forms — whole or sliced — were used by a few more creative housewives in the 1970s, when recipes for casseroles began to fill the pages of women's magazines. Tinned mushrooms were used to 'perk up a meal'. One respondent wrote: 'I seem to remember my dad saying that mushrooms were fancy food.'[5] From this we can see that it wasn't just a question of whether mushrooms were food or non-food, they were also an indicator of social class. Mushrooms were a fashion symbol, something that people further up the social ladder were familiar with and didn't think twice about eating.

City folk, vicars, teachers, well-educated ladies, or artists who were ahead of their time — these were the sort of people who might be seen carrying a mushroom basket. They represented Norway's mycological avant-garde at that time. The joy of mushrooms was much the same then as it is now. A woman from Rygge wrote:

We have always been great field guide users and we eventually learned to identify a good many different mushrooms. We never took risks, and if we were in any doubt we would go to the food advisory bureau or to people we knew to be well-versed in mushrooms. I remember from when I was around 10 or 12, my dad standing at the old stove, blanching mushrooms in a big pot. We children (four of us) stood around him, waiting to taste whatever it was that smelled so good. In the evening, after a little expedition, there would be crispy, fried mushrooms, or stewed mushrooms in a cream sauce, with Dad as the proud cook. There were several benefits to be had from these mushroom gathering expeditions: fresh air, exercise, sights, sounds, and food for the table ... When the children were small we always took a primus stove, a frying pan, margarine, and salt with us, and then we could have a lovely little taste of what the forest had to offer. It was such fun to eat crisp, fried mushrooms straight from the pan with our fingers ...[6]

When people hear that I pick mushrooms, I almost always get the same response. They proceed to tell me a story of some mushroom poisoning incident, more often than not of a whole dinner party ending up in dialysis after ingesting toxic mushrooms. The subtext is clear: 'Yep, dangerous things, mushrooms.'

'Why bother picking mushrooms when you can buy them

in the shops?' mushroom sceptics will no doubt ask. Presumably only a very few would pick pieces of mushroom off a bought pizza because they've heard that mushrooms can be poisonous, but the number of people who associate them mainly with rot and mould seems to have remained both large and unchanging throughout Norwegian history.

The helpline of Norway's National Poisons Information Centre receives around 40,000 calls a year. The proportion of calls regarding different types of inquiry has remained much the same for years: around 40 per cent of all inquiries relate to technical and/or chemical products, around 40 per cent to medicines, approximately 10 per cent to 'miscellaneous', and about 10 per cent have to do with plants, animals, and fungi. In other words, not many people call to ask about poisoning due to mushrooms. When it comes to mushroom poisoning, the gap between reality and fantasy is pretty wide, particularly among mycophobes (people who hate mushrooms).

The difference between mycophiles (mushroom lovers) and mycophobes is as stark as that between night and day. The mycophile endeavours to minimise the risk by adopting an extremely cautious approach to mushroom picking — 'defensive mushrooming' — and by continually increasing their knowledge. To the mycophobe, mushrooms are the death that lurks in the forest. All they see is the danger of poisoning, life-long dialysis, or worse. Mycophobes regard mushroom picking as an extreme sport, and the eating of self-picked mushrooms — regardless of the picker's level of expertise — as an irresponsible act involving great risk, a bit like playing Russian roulette. The mycophobe's last resort is the 'human error' card. However knowledgeable and careful you are, accidents can always happen. And what can one say to that, except that the mycophobe is right: the risk of poisoning can never be reduced to zero. Even mushroom experts can make mistakes. If you eat wild mushrooms there is no way you can guard against poisoning completely. But even mycophobes would agree that there is also an element of risk involved in getting into a car, or in going home with someone you've just met on a fun night out in town. They may even indulge in activities which contribute more to the injury and accident statistics than the well-informed consumption of mushrooms. My conclusion is that it's not the actual element of recklessness that lies behind the mycophobe's aversion to mushrooms. That is just an excuse, a way of disguising their fear as the simple, sensible avoidance of dangerous behaviour. I can tell a mycophobe a mile off, long before they've finished their moral tale of the disastrous family dinner. In such situations I keep my mouth shut and try to keep smiling, although I'm really not interested in carrying on talking to a mycophobe who views mushrooming as a hobby on a par with keeping poisonous snakes as pets.

In the nineteenth century, when mushrooms first began to appear on the dining table, it was primarily in the homes of the well-educated. This contrasted sharply with the picture in most other countries. Dr Olav Johan Sopp (a pioneer within Norwegian mycology who changed his name from J. Oluf Olsen in order to highlight his great passion, 'sopp' being the

Norwegian word for mushrooms and fungi) wrote in *Spiselig Sop* (*Edible Fungi*) (1883) that elsewhere in the world it was the poor who gathered, ate and sold mushrooms. In Norway, on the other hand, it was the fashionable élite, who had eaten mushrooms on their travels out into the world, i.e. Europe, in elegant restaurants and at grand society gatherings. They brought this sophisticated gastronomic habit home with them to Norway. But those who had never left the old country, who were often less enlightened, with little in the way of education, tended to be sceptical about what they saw as the gentry's snobbish eating habits, not least among them their penchant for mushrooms.

These days, when I meet a mycophobe, I tell myself that the person concerned probably comes from a poor farming family of simple habits. He might boast a university degree, a good job or a smart home address, but to my mind such hidebound mycophobic attitudes tell another story. Generations of prejudice, ignorance and lack of curiosity have fostered strong and irrational feelings, and these have boiled down to a hard stock cube that I cannot dissolve. I have neither the patience nor the inclination to save mycophobes who have already made up their minds that mushrooms are more dangerous than wolves and synonymous with deadly poison. That's their problem. My own feeling, when I meet such people, is as follows: the more mycophobes, the more mushrooms for the rest of us. I'm not as patient as Dr Sopp, who worked indefatigably to spread the good news about fungi, but I take comfort in the fact that the potato, which was introduced to Norway in 1758, also 'met here with great misgiving: people most certainly did not want to use it, far less grow it.'

Which mushrooms are edible?

As a newcomer to the mushrooming community, I was surprised to discover that a list of standards for the edibility of mushrooms is actually a Norwegian invention. The List of Standards for the Nutritional Value of Norwegian Mushrooms was first drawn up in 2000. To mushroom experts in Norway its word is law, and mushroom inspectors follow its guidelines to the letter. This list sprang from a desire to establish a common code of practice and thus avoid a situation in which answers on the edibility of a particular mushroom could vary from checkpoint to checkpoint. Some inspectors might privately believe that one mushroom is a genuine 'three-star' gem, while others consider it totally tasteless. The list of standards was designed to regulate this disparity by splitting the mushrooms brought in for inspection into four categories: 1) edible, 2) non-comestible, 3) toxic, and 4) highly toxic.

The list is regularly updated in line with new research findings and this can lead to certain mushrooms once considered toxic being acquitted, so to speak. The Luxuriant Ringstalk, *Stropharia hornemannii*, is a case in point. Recent research has also led to certain species which were previously regarded as edible, like the Honey Fungus, *Armillaria mellea*, and the Yellow Knight, *Tricholoma equestre*, now being rated as toxic.

On one occasion, my mushroom buddy K. and I found a large colony of Red-Banded Webcap, *Cortinarius armillatus*, in the forest. We both knew that this species is now categorised as 'non-comestible' on the list of standards, but we both also knew of a number of the Society's old guard who had been eating this mushroom 'for years' and were still eating it, unfazed by the List's latest updates because they had 'only ever had good experiences' with it. K. had just read on Swedish social media that some people have hailed the Red-Banded Webcap as the best mushroom of them all. K. announced therefore that he was going to get to the truth of it, once and for all. His family were away, so he could put it to the test without putting their lives and health at risk. I helped him pick the Webcaps and he soon had a basketful of fresh, supple specimens. He went home pleased and happy and ready to do his bit in the service of mushrooming.

Later that evening I sent him a text, asking how the mushrooms had tasted. No, he hadn't eaten them yet, but he was going to have them tomorrow. I texted him again the next day and received an immediate reply. He had eaten the mushrooms and thought they were pretty good. It turned out that K. had had to steel himself to carry out his mission, so great is the psychological hold exerted by the List of Standards. In any case, I was left not knowing what to think about the List. My curiosity had been aroused.

Cortinarius armillatus, Red-Banded Webcap

Why, for example, was it necessary to differentiate between 'toxic' and 'highly toxic'? The reason I had been given was that *all* the mushrooms in a basket had to be discarded if they had come into contact with a mushroom from the 'highly toxic' category, but that such drastic action was not necessary if the offending mushroom was only considered 'toxic'. And, with K.'s experience with the Red-Banded Webcap still fresh in my memory, what defines those mushrooms that were clearly regarded as neither edible nor toxic/highly toxic — the ones categorised as 'non-comestible'?

On the Association's website it says that the definition 'non-comestible' was arrived at on the basis of taste and/or consistency. That the experts who manage the list might not like the Almond Woodwax, *Hygrophorus agathosmus*, because it smells bad is one thing. Whether it is edible is another matter entirely. A little bit of googling reveals that this mushroom can be eaten. Some people think it even has an 'almondy' flavour. It is now on my list of mushrooms to be tasted. All of this makes me think that my preferences in terms of taste and consistency may differ somewhat from those who have the final say on updates to the List of Standards.

I don't remember the first time I heard about the annual mushroom festival in Telluride, Colorado, but what I do remember are the pictures from the festival parade, with everyone in some sort of mushroom-themed fancy dress. It all looked pretty crazy and weird, but that was exactly what appealed to me. This was one mushroom festival I really fancied attending. So when, one year, I finally got the chance to go to the Telluride Mushroom Festival, I jumped at it. It was in Telluride that I first ate some young Shingled Hedgehog, *Sarcodon imbricatus*, a mushroom which, according to the List of Standards, is not considered comestible. So I was a little baffled to find that I really enjoyed the robust Shingled Hedgehog soup.

I brought this issue up with my local society's more experienced members and was told that, while certain mushrooms may be edible, they can be small and hence not worth the effort to gather for food. Other mushrooms end up in the 'non-comestible' category because there is some uncertainty as to whether they are toxic.

Clearly, there are many reasons why edible mushrooms may be consigned to the 'non-comestible' category. I was informed that the List of Standards is, first and foremost, a manual for practical mushroom inspection, in a situation where there is often little time to go into detail. The queue of people wishing to have their mushrooms checked can sometimes be very long.

It is, however, a fact that for interested mushroom gatherers the List of Standards provides the most up-to-date information on the edibility of the most common species.

It is neither the aim nor the point of the List of Standards to act as the mushroom police or arbiter of taste, but in effect this is what has happened. Although comments have been entered against certain mushrooms which fall into the 'non-comestible' category, a few of these seem pretty perfunctory. With several species, for example, all it says in the comment box is: 'unpleasant smell or taste'. But perceptions of smell and taste are, as we know, highly subjective. Furthermore, some mushrooms may not taste good when fried, but are excellent when prepared in other ways. An expanded version of the List of Standards, one based not on subjective likes and dislikes, would, therefore, not go amiss. This would provide people with enough information to make up their *own* minds as to whether they like the taste and/or consistency of an edible mushroom or not. Then it would also be up to the individual to decide whether to pick a very small edible mushroom when gathering enough for just a modest meal will take a lot of time and effort. But the last word on this matter has not yet been said — the question as to what ought to be included on the List of Standards is a highly emotive topic within the mushroom community.

In limbo

One of anthropology's contributions to the general understanding of society is the term *rite de passage*, coined by Dutchman Arnold van Gennep in 1909 to describe a ritual marking a new defined stage in a person's life. Christenings, confirmations, weddings, and funerals are all rites of passage. Van Gennep uses a house as a metaphor for society, with the many rooms of the house representing different social sub-groups. According to van Gennep, an individual goes through three phases on their way from one room to another. Separation (from a group), incorporation (in a new group), and the liminal phase, when they are neither in the old or the new group.

The Latin word *līmen* means 'threshold' or 'boundary'. From the same root comes the word 'limbo' — in the Roman Catholic Church, the name for a region somewhere between Heaven and Hell. Here languish those souls who have not been granted the joy of eternal life in Heaven with God and are trapped in no man's land: they may have escaped being sent to Hell, but the Pearly Gates are also closed to them.

I was married, and then, suddenly, I was a widow. So far, my journey through the labyrinth of mourning had been one long, unbroken liminal phase. I was nowhere.

In the liminal phase, everything that is familiar, everything you take for granted, crumbles and becomes unclear. You are thrown a third-class ticket for a journey into the unknown, a journey which can at times be turbulent, and is certainly never pleasant.

Everything is in flux and all options are, in theory, open — a situation which allows scope for positive transformation. But it takes a lot just to stay upright in this alien lunar landscape. The waves of emotion that roil and moil inside you when you are in limbo are extreme: anger over an unwanted situation, longing for your old life, and fear of the new. They make it hard to glimpse new doors opening.

Angry at the grass

I'm angry at the grass, angry at the lawnmower. I push the old mechanical mower back and forth, back and forth across the tiny patch of grass at the allotment. Are the blades dull again already, after one winter? They were sharpened only last summer by a friend, in exchange for an al fresco dinner. Eiolf liked cutting the grass, but what he liked most of all was trimming the edges, using a whole arsenal of tools I didn't know the names of. I ram the mower into the cottage wall again and again rather than get out the trimmer. And of course the edges are anything but neat. And of course my mother gets annoyed at my futile efforts to use the lawnmower as a battering ram. What door I'm attempting to open is a mystery to me. Amazingly, she keeps her mouth shut and leaves me alone.

Looking back on it, anger was not the dominant emotion after Eiolf's death. Is that because I'm not religious and therefore had no god to be angry with? I certainly wasn't angry with Eiolf. Apart from the all-pervading sadness, the one feeling that kept welling up was gratitude. I was so grateful to have had Eiolf as my mate. But I had been told by psychologist friends that anger is a vital part of the grieving process. Was I doing it wrong?

April Fool

It's 1 April, but no one has tried to trick me.

If Eiolf were here he would have come up with something.

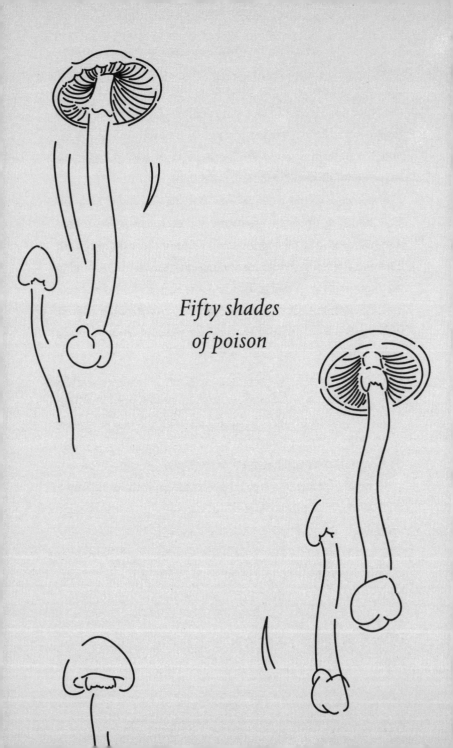

*Fifty shades
of poison*

There's a story of an adulterous couple on a romantic weekend in the mountains who had to be rushed to the intensive care unit at a local hospital after eating what they mistook for some lovely wild mushrooms. The man had told his wife he was attending a seminar to do with his work, while the woman was supposedly away with some women friends. Their cover stories were blown, however, when their respective spouses and families met at the hospital. What was worse for these two, one wonders: to be hovering between life and death due to mushroom poisoning or to have had their affair discovered?

A lot of people are intrigued by the poisonous aspect of mushrooms. There is a widely held idea that one bite of a toxic mushroom spells almost instant death: the victim throwing up over the dinner table, foaming at the mouth, or something equally dramatic. That was pretty much how I saw it too, but I have since learned that poison in mushrooms can be many things. There are numerous different types of mycotoxin. Not all toxic mushrooms cause permanent renal failure or premature death. Poison in mushrooms is not like pregnancy; no one can be 'a little bit pregnant', you either are or you aren't. But not all poisonous mushrooms are *equally* toxic. Some are just *a little bit* toxic.

Of all the hundreds of thousands of species in the world, only a handful of mushrooms are deadly poisonous. Ingestion of these poisonous compounds gives rise to a variety of symptoms and outcomes. Amatoxins, present in the Death Cap, the Destroying Angel, and the Funeral Bell, *Galerina marginata*, which all grow in Norway, attack the liver and are lethal even in small doses. The Death Cap and the Destroying Angel are responsible for approximately 90 per cent of all fatal cases of mushroom poisoning in the world. Naturally, these (and their lookalikes) are covered by all beginners' courses on mushrooms. Other mycotoxins attack the central nervous system or the intestines, and it has recently been shown that mushroom poisoning may also lead to a muscle syndrome known as rhabdomyolisis in which skeletal muscle is broken down. Another condition, hemolysis, involves the rupturing of red blood cells.

Mycotoxic reactions can be classified according to the time it takes for symptoms to manifest themselves. The Deadly Webcap, *Cortinarius rubellus*, contains a mycotoxin called orellanine, which is harmful to the liver and kidneys. Even a very small amount can prove fatal. But the effects of the poison may not be felt for anything up to two weeks. In other words, you can be going around, blissfully unaware, and then suddenly your kidneys cease to function. Generally, though, it's safe to say that cases of mushroom poisoning which produce an immediate effect in the form of vomiting, diarrhoea, and retching are the least dangerous. The worst damage is usually done by mycotoxins that have a longer latent phase, which is to say, the time that elapses between ingestion of the mushroom and the appearance of the first signs of poisoning. Even with a mushroom that is regarded as 'deadly poisonous' lives can be saved if the right treatment is forthcoming soon enough.

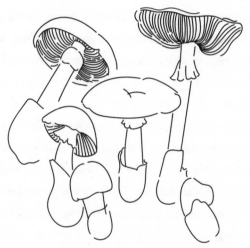

Amanita phalloides, Death Cap

Is it possible to tell just by looking at it whether a mushroom is poisonous? I've been told more than once by strangers that the mushrooms in my basket 'look poisonous'. But notions of what constitutes a poisonous appearance are subjective. My hypothesis is that anything that doesn't resemble what people are used to seeing in the shops looks poisonous to a mycophobe. If your point of reference is the white button mushroom from the supermarket then something like the Lurid Bolete, *Suillellus luridus*, may well look pretty inedible, with its reddish-brown meshwork on the stem and its yellow flesh, which stains blue when bruised or broken. I've often picked Lurid Boletes as big as dinner plates for the mushroom stall at the Farmer's Market in Oslo, where this species is immediately cast as the 'monster mushroom'. Everyone always wants to know if it's poisonous. I just give them a big smile and cheerfully inform them that it's actually delicious when well-cooked. It's always hilarious to see their reactions, but it's hard to say whether this information is enough to shatter their idea of how a poisonous mushroom should look.

There are also any number of misconceptions regarding the supposed identifying features of poisonous mushrooms. For example, that poisonous mushrooms never grow on trees, or that all poisonous mushrooms are brightly coloured. Some people even believe that mushrooms eaten by insects or animal can't be poisonous, or that silver will tarnish if brought into contact with toxic mushrooms. The fact is, however, that there are certain substances which are poisonous to people, but not to animals, and there's no point in taking a silver spoon on mushrooming expeditions because the silver's reaction says nothing about a mushroom's potential toxicity. Sadly, when it comes to poison there are no short cuts. We simply have to learn every mushroom by heart, so we will always recognise them, like old friends. You never mistake the face of a good friend, no matter whether they're having a good day or a bad one. It's the same with mushrooms.

Sometimes they are tiny, lovely, and delicate. Sometimes specimens of the same species can be old, gnarled, and ugly.

A friend who had recently run a course for beginners was able to report that people vary widely in their ability to tell different mushrooms apart. When he presented the class with a chanterelle and a Deadly Webcap, one person spotted the difference straight away, while another said they looked alike because they were 'both yellow'. The Norwegian Poison Information Centre has also seen instances of good edible mushrooms like the Penny Bun and the Hedgehog Mushroom being confused with the Destroying Angel, even though they are totally different in terms of colour, shape, and other features. The relevant distinctions simply have to be learned. Memory plays a vital part in how we perceive things, and memory is based on learning and practice. The more experience and knowledge you acquire, the better equipped you are to spot the little details that matter. Because initial standpoints can vary, some people may have to work a little harder than others, but, where mushrooms are concerned, knowing the crucial distinctions can spell the difference between life and death.

A typical beginner mistake is to place too much trust in book illustrations, since a mushroom's appearance can vary greatly depending on its age and other factors. It can be easy, when eager to make a positive identification, to focus on the similarities between a picture in a book and a mushroom in the wild and overlook the dissimilarities. It's really all about hands-on experience. When it comes to mushroom expertise, practice make perfect. It's like learning a trade. Skill increases slowly and organically. Order gradually emerges from chaos.

But it's not simple.

The Deadly Webcap, rather condescendingly referred to by Norwegian mushroomers as the 'Sandefjord chanterelle', is one of the most toxic mushrooms found in the Norwegian countryside, and it sometimes grows alongside another chanterelle, the Funnel chanterelle. More experienced mushroom gatherers find it hard to understand how anyone could confuse the Deadly Webcap with the Funnel chanterelle when, to them, these two species look so different. Rumour has it that someone in Sandefjord — or possibly some other place — once mistook a Deadly Webcap for a chanterelle and wound up on a dialysis machine for the rest of their life.

Cortinarius rubellus, Deadly Webcap

S., a well-known figure in Norwegian mushroom circles, once picked a bunch of superb Prince mushrooms to serve to some French visitors to Norway, only to be told that they would not touch them. This came as a surprise to him. In Norway, the Prince mushroom is not only regarded as edible, many people consider it the best wild mushroom in the country. In the days when a star system was used to rate mushrooms, the Prince was given the top rating of three stars. The French think differently, however. Didier Borgarino, author of the acclaimed French field guide to mushrooms, *Champignons de Provence*, lists only two members of the *Agaricus* genus as edible: the Meadow Mushroom, *Agaricus campestris*, and the Scaly Wood Mushroom, *Agaricus langei*. This will no doubt surprise those in Norway who know their mushrooms. According to Borgarino, to be on the safe side it is best to throw away all Prince mushrooms, Horse mushrooms, and Scaly Wood mushrooms, since these species can accumulate high quantities of cadmium and other heavy metals. Mushroom gatherers in Norway are well aware of this fact and are careful, therefore, to restrict their consumption of them. But many French mycologists go even further and refrain completely from eating these mushrooms or their shop-bought equivalents.

My jaw dropped when I heard this. I could well imagine that individual preferences as to taste might differ, what I hadn't expected, though, was that there would be different opinions regarding the questions of toxicity or edibility. I had been under the impression that these were absolutes, on which everyone agreed. Didn't all countries employ the same list of edible and toxic mushrooms?

What I have learned is that there can be lots of reasons why someone might feel unwell after eating mushrooms.

One thing is the size of the portion. Sometimes you can have too much of a good thing. Even so-called healthy foods can be poisonous if you eat too much of them. We know that salt is absolutely essential to the regulation of our bodily functions, but it is bad for us if we take too much of it. The same is true of water. As Paracelsus, the father of toxicology, put it so neatly in the sixteenth century: the only difference between a poison and a medicine is the dose. If someone becomes ill after eating mushrooms, it is not necessarily because they have been poisoned; with mushrooms, as with other things, moderation is a virtue. And if you are not in the best of health to start with, eating unusually large amounts of mushrooms is not recommended, even when they are certified as edible. The Association warns against eating mushrooms as a main ingredient in a meal several times a day for two or more days in succession.

In addition to the dose, one has to allow for individual allergic reactions. One man's perfect mushroom can provoke an allergic reaction in another. Not necessarily with fatal consequences, but causing temporary discomfort, nausea, and stomach trouble.

Another common cause of mushroom poisoning is incorrect preparation; some mushrooms are toxic when raw, but perfectly all right to eat when properly cooked. In Norway, the mushroom which most frequently induces a bad reaction after ingestion is not a toxic species but an edible one, the Orange Birch Bolete. This mushroom is easily recognisable, with its hipster 'stubble' on the stem and its fleshy, brick-red cap. For many years, the Orange Birch Bolete was included on the 'six safe mushrooms' list. The list was later renamed the 'five safe mushrooms' when the Orange Birch Bolete was removed from it — not because it is poisonous in itself, but because there have been cases of illness due to undercooking of this mushroom. The Orange Birch Bolete also grows in the hills, and one can easily imagine hungry hikers getting a bit impatient once they're gathered round the campfire. As a general rule, all mushrooms, including those from the supermarket, should be properly cooked. There are those who might protest and point to all the shop-bought mushrooms they've eaten raw in salads since the 1970s and 1980s, but the fact is that even shop-bought varieties contain phenylhydrazine derivatives, which are potentially carcinogenic, but which are destroyed when subjected to heat.

It is also worth mentioning that the fear of mushroom poisoning itself can cause dizziness, headaches, and stomach ache. So sensitive souls who have their doubts about mushrooms should avoid eating them altogether.

Mushroom inspectors are obliged to reject the entire contents of a basket of edible mushrooms if one highly toxic mushroom is found among them. Most mushroom gatherers accept this once they have been told that one Deadly Webcap the size of a sugar cube is enough to kill a person. Absurdly, however, there is always someone who objects when told that their chanterelles will have to be thrown away. On one occasion, a mushroom expert I know found five large Destroying Angels among some lovely Penny Buns in a plastic bag that had been brought in for checking. The Penny Buns were covered in bits of the friable Destroying Angels. The man who had handed in the plastic bag was not at all pleased when the inspector gave him the bad news and was all set to run off with the tainted Penny Buns. My friend had to use all his diplomatic wiles to get the bag back so that the entire contents could be destroyed.

According to the Norwegian Poison Information Service, most cases of poisoning occur in adults. Although they receive many inquiries concerning children every year, children rarely eat much of any mushroom they come across in the wild; while children will nibble the mushrooms they find, adults make entire meals of them. The classic nightmare scenario is that of an amateur who mistakes a toxic mushroom for what he thinks is a delicacy and invites family and friends to a slap-up meal. Unfortunately, many immigrants to Norway fall into this category. More than half of those who have suffered serious mushroom poisoning in recent years were of immigrant background. Often these individuals will find a mushroom in the Norwegian countryside which bears a resemblance to a good, safe mushroom from their own country and celebrate this great discovery with a big dinner. One such unfortunate mix-up can occur between young Death Caps and the Asian Paddy Straw Mushroom, *Volvariella volvacea*. Similarly, the Destroying Angel can be mistaken for another white mushroom, the Chepang Slender Caesar, *Amanita chepangiana*, a native of South-East Asia. The Destroying Angel doesn't taste or smell particularly bad, so people have no inkling that anything might be wrong. Even in small doses, the Destroying Angel can cause damage to the liver cells. And, if the antidote doesn't work, this can lead to liver failure and, at worst, death.

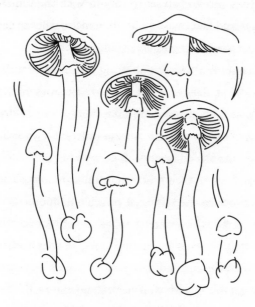

Amanita virosa, Destroying Angels

Establishing the facts about mushroom poisoning is, for many obvious reasons, not easy. One key reason for this is that the culprit has not always been kept and positively identified. Nonetheless, the figures from the Norwegian Poison Information Service do provide some clues. These show that in the period 2010–2014 hospitals in Norway recorded 43 admissions on strong suspicion of serious mushroom poisoning. In all cases, those admitted were adults, and, over the five-year period, one fatality was recorded, due to ingestion of Destroying Angel. The Destroying Angel was also the mushroom most frequently mistaken for something else during that five-year timeframe. It's hard to understand why the majority of people in Norway recognise and know to steer clear of the Fly Agaric, when it is the seemingly innocent Destroying Angel which poses the greatest real danger.

Sometimes mushroom poisoning is the result of downright stupidity. I was flabbergasted to hear the story of a group of teenage boys who attempted to get high on what they hoped were Liberty Caps, or magic mushrooms, *Psilocybe semilanceata*. One lazy summer day they found some mushrooms in a meadow and egged each other on to eat as many as they could, trying to produce the strongest possible hallucinogenic effect. As it happened, they weren't magic mushrooms, but luckily for them they weren't poisonous either, so they suffered no ill effects. Nevertheless, indulging in such recklessness is tantamount to gambling with your health and can easily land you in intensive care. I recently heard another story, about a man who called a mushroom expert to tell him that he had been eating the Sheathed Woodtuft, *Pholiota mutabilis*, all his life, but had just discovered that it has a deadly lookalike: the Funeral Bell. The Funeral Bell contains a cytotoxin which can induce life-threatening changes in the function of liver and kidney cells.

'What should I do about the "Sheathed Woodtuft" that I've just eaten?' the caller wanted to know. The fate of this man, who was clearly blessed more with good luck than good judgement, is not known.

In other countries, too, one encounters misconceptions regarding mycotoxins. I happened to be in America when the Museum of Natural History in New York was staging a major exhibition on the role of natural poisons in mythology and medicine. As always, everything is so much bigger and more spectacular in the United States. The entrance to the exhibition looked like a clearing in a tropical forest. We could hear the sounds of the jungle and were told by guides that we should expect to see poisonous snakes, poisonous scorpions, poisonous ants, and some of the strongest poisons nature has to offer. We were introduced to poisonous frogs in glass cases and a tree whose sap is so toxic that you ought not to stand under when it rains — if you do you risk contracting eczema from the 'toxic rain'. Nowhere, though, was there any sign of poisonous mushrooms. When I asked a guide about this I was directed to a full-scale model of Shakespeare's three witches from *Macbeth*, cooking up their hellish broth from all manner of foul ingredients. This being America, the home of Hollywood, no scenographic effect had been spared. Smoke curled up from the witches' cauldron as they muttered their secret spells. At the foot of one of the witches sat a small, plastic Fly Agaric. 'Here you can see a False Morel,' the lady said. I was sorry to have to inform her that this pathetic little plastic blob was, in fact, a Fly

Agaric and not a False Morel. My great respect for this museum, which housed the most wonderful dinosaurs in the city and in which the renowned anthropologist Margaret Meade once had her office, evaporated like mycotoxins in boiling water. One could actually mount an exhibition devoted solely to mushroom poisons in nature, mythology, and medicine, but that thought had clearly never occurred to the curator of this exhibition. Nor did the museum need to make arduous expeditions to South America to collect and bring back poisonous animals and plants — all they had to do was to stroll out of the main door and go mushroom hunting in Central Park.

Not black and white

Since taste is not only an individual matter, but also culturally determined, it seemed only natural to me that opinions might differ from country to country when it came to the 'edible' and 'non-comestible' categories. What I hadn't expected, though, was to discover international variations regarding the 'toxic' category. I discovered, for example, that one mushroom which is considered poisonous in Norway, the Amethyst Deceiver, is both sold and *eaten* as a matter of course in other countries. And there are examples of the opposite, too. What are we supposed to make of all this?

I visited Professor Klaus Høiland at the University of Oslo, hoping to be enlightened. He chuckled and began by saying that, when it comes to poisons in mushrooms, the picture is not black-and-white, but more a *fifty shades* kind of thing. While mushroom experts all over the world are in agreement as far as the truly deadly fungi are concerned, many species evidently fall into a grey zone. Contrary to what I, as a mushroom novice, naïvely imagined, it's not as simple as all that to determine whether a mushroom is poisonous or not. I found this both shocking and intriguing.

Many veteran mushroomers wax nostalgic about the days when you could eat a Yellow Knight in peace. Since then, the Yellow Knight has been moved from the 'edible' to the 'toxic' category on the List of Standards, a change prompted by a number of cases of fatal poisoning in France — after the consumption of large quantities of the mushroom at several successive meals, it should be said. Hyper-sensitivity to a substance can be built up over a period of time and there are also differences when it comes to individual predisposition to Yellow Knight poisoning. But until exonerated by further research this mushroom will be excluded from the List of Standards' 'edible' category.

'Is anyone doing research into this?' I asked the mycologists.

I was informed that no research is currently being done into this subject in Norway, but none of the experts I asked seemed particularly concerned about this. In any case the practical conclusion was clear: as long as the mushroom was under investigation, it would remain off the List of Standards' 'edible' category and, hence, be given the thumbs-down by mushroom inspectors.

I had heard stories of how tasty the Yellow Knight was, but hadn't thought much about them until the day when I suddenly came upon my first Yellow Knights in the woods east of Oslo — a small cluster of them, beautiful, yellow, upright, and elegant, they stood there in a little clump. Its Latin epithet is *equestre*, meaning a horseman, and it's easy to see why it is also known as 'Man on Horseback'. I found myself in a dilemma: to eat or not to eat? Feeling a little shaky I took the mushrooms home and posted a message on social media, asking whether anyone had tried Yellow Knights. I immediately received a number of positive replies. So I took my courage in both hands and fried and ate one mushroom. It was good. When I told some friends who weren't mushroom enthusiasts about this, they asked me what I would have done if they had brought a whole basket of prime Yellow Knights for inspection. There is no doubt that I would have rejected them, but would I have tucked them 'under the table' for my own consumption? Fortunately, I have never been put in that rather tricky situation.

The French take a restrictive approach to wild mushrooms in general due to the danger from cadmium and other heavy metals. How dangerous the levels of cadmium in mushrooms native to Norway are can no doubt be debated, but in all probability it's not mushrooms, but tobacco, that is the biggest source of cadmium accumulation in the population. And as far as I know, smokers don't die of cadmium poisoning, but from other causes.

The attitude to Russula mushrooms in the UK is different from than that in Norway. I was surprised to learn that Russulas are seldom eaten there. One of the most popular British field guides, *Mushrooms* by John Wright, advises the eating of only five Russula mushrooms (the Charcoal Burner, *Russula cyanoxantha*, the Quilted Green Russula, *Russula virescens*, the Common Yellow Russula, *Russula ochroleuca*, the Yellow Swamp Russula, *Russula claroflava*, and the Powdery Brittlegill, *Russula parazurea*). But, since many people find it difficult to identify these five, the rule of thumb followed by local societies, such as the Dorset Fungus Group, is to stick to the Charcoal Burner. When I joined the group on their annual trip to Brownsea Island, they told me how people from the Baltic countries ate far more members of the Russula family and how they had the odd habit of tasting the raw mushrooms to decide whether they were edible. They ate the mild-tasting ones and threw away the bitter ones. I said that we practised the 'Baltic method' in Norway too. Maybe it was just my imagination, but I thought they gave me some funny looks when I told them about this foolhardy Norwegian Russula test.

Even between two such close neighbours as Norway and Sweden, national perceptions and practice vary widely. Take the webcap family, for instance: in Norway we steer well clear of all webcaps (except for the Gypsy Mushroom, *Cortinarius caperatus*), while the Swedes think nothing of tucking into the Birch Webcap, *Cortinarius triumphans*, and other webcaps. I've seen proud Swedes posting boastful photographs of baskets full of Birch Webcaps and Red-Banded Webcaps on social media — mushrooms which would be rejected without hesitation at Norwegian inspection checkpoints.

The reverse is also true. For example: the small, but beautiful Amethyst Deceiver, *Laccaria amethystina*, is eaten in Norway, but considered inedible by the Swedes, who believe that it contains arsenic. Here in Norway I even have a recipe for Amethyst Deceiver, given to me by a respected veteran mushroomer. Besides the Amethyst Deceiver, the ingredients for this recipe, entitled Bewitched Mushrooms, include Waxy Laccaria, *Laccaria laccata*, young chanterelles and Funnel chanterelles, vermouth, cinnamon, and cloves. In Norway, no one worries about the danger of arsenic in Amethyst Deceivers. Bewitched Mushrooms are used as a tangy garnish for ice cream or other desserts. If you come from a home with a more relaxed attitude to alcohol you could even serve it to children.

You would think it would be a simple matter to find out whether the Amethyst Deceiver actually does contain arsenic. Or, *if* it does, whether the amount of arsenic it contains makes it dangerous to eat. Likewise, you might expect that it would be easy to determine whether it's actually safe for Norwegians to eat the Red-Banded Webcap or the Birch Webcap — since the Swedes have no problem with them. Whatever the case, it seems that the question as to whether a mushroom is edible or toxic is not merely a question of which actual poison it contains, but what the national *attitude* is to different potential toxins.

I have observed two approaches which illustrate different risk analysis strategies: in Norway, some people will only pick mushrooms in the woods or fields, to minimise the risk of ingesting cadmium, while others argue that nowadays one ought also to think twice about picking mushrooms from the central reservations on motorways. Others adopt a middle way, removing the gills before cooking, since this is where the cadmium tends to accumulate. I've not been able to confirm whether this last tactic works, but here we are clearly entering a grey area where different nations and different individuals have varying notions regarding the risk of poisoning. At the end of the day, though, it's up to the individual mushroom gatherer to decide what risk they're prepared to take.

In my own case, the Prince mushroom, shunned in France, is a personal favourite. From my very first bite I was sold. And since I'm a non-smoker, my cadmium levels were presumably low to start with, so this is not something I worry about at all. Compared to the Prince, shop-bought mushrooms are tasteless, lacking in character, and 'unsexy'. Besides which, shop-bought mushrooms have no smell, while, to my nose, edible mushrooms from the wild have a wonderful almondy scent. Sweet, almost biscuity.

Flow

There was nothing Eiolf liked better than weeding at the allotment. He could spend hours out there, with no music in his ears, no connection to the Internet's countless distractions. When he was weeding, he gave himself up to it completely. He was a virtuoso in the art of being in the moment, in the flow. Maybe that is why little children and animals always came to him.

Am I idealising Eiolf, now that he's gone? I suppose I am, since that's how it is to remember things through the prism of loss. Some details are magnified, others vanish from view. One thing is certain, though: unlike me, he wasn't always rushing from one meeting to the next, from one task to the next. He was quietly present wherever he was. To quote someone close to us: I was in charge of action and implementation, Eiolf was the cool, relaxed one.

When longed-for rain finally fell on Oslo everything in my postage stamp of a garden ran riot. There was no way I could put off doing the weeding. But to my surprise it was a very pleasant job, much better than I had expected. It wasn't as boring as I had feared. In fact, it was good to just do one thing. It was nice to sit on the soft grass, to smell the scent of the garden peonies, the mock orange and wild marjoram, hear the faint hum of bumble bees and see the butterflies flitting about, while up above the whirling propellers of air ambulances signalled that help was on the way. Having discovered the delights of weeding, I have come to the conclusion that as a form of bereavement therapy it is greatly underrated. Not only because it is a concrete task and you have something to show for it right away, but because new experiences await you when you stop fighting it and actually choose to do the weeding. In fact you may actually see things with fresh eyes, and in so doing become a new person.

This made me think about mushroom trails and how, if you take the same path back as you took on the way out, the light falls differently, enabling you to spot mushrooms you had simply walked past earlier — and sometimes a real prize at that. The composer John Cage was also a keen mushroom hunter. He compared the experience of finding a well-concealed mushroom to that of listening to beautiful, soft sounds, a quiet symphony, one which is often drowned out by the clamour of everyday life. A new angle can offer new mushrooming possibilities and experiences when you least expect them.

It's not unusual to come home from a mushrooming expedition with an empty basket. But it doesn't stop me going out there, not just to try my luck, as it were, but because even a more or less mushroom-less trip is worthwhile. I always start out with high hopes, armed with my biggest basket. But sometimes, after a while, I realise that I'll have to be content with getting something else out of my trip. It might be that I'll find a 'mycologically interesting' fungus, or come upon a stretch of woodland which would be worth returning to later in the season, or maybe I manage to take a great picture of a particular mushroom. Like big-game hunters, mushroom hunters shoot photographs non-stop when their prey is within reach. Selfies taken together with a fantastic haul of mushrooms are a common motif in mushrooming circles. These photographs are our hunting trophies. But even fruitless expeditions are good, because they get you out and about. So the joy of mushrooming is not confined to a brimming basket. It is, as I have discovered, much more than that.

The point, when you go mushroom hunting, is not to cover as many miles as you can as quickly as possible. One of my friends, who uses the Runkeeper app to track those sites where he has found the best mushrooms and to find his way back to the car park, is often teased by colleagues at work, who use this same app to track how far and how fast they run. My friend's Runkeeper log looks like a big scribble. The mushroom lesson for the new widow is that specific GPS coordinates are not the only thing you need when you go mushroom hunting. Having the right attitude is just as important. Above all else, it pays just to 'be', to focus on the moment. Do that and you will expand the definition of happiness.

The question of where to find mushrooms can be answered in three short words: in the forest. But such an answer is of no help to a poor layperson who is interested in learning more. If you don't want to give away your GPS details, but would still like to help, it's best to say something like: go for a walk in a nearby forest. As you meet the forest and the forest meets you, try to leave behind all the hurly-burly of daily life and concentrate, instead, on tuning in to the rhythm and frequency of the forest. Let it become a part of you. Then you will relax, your pulse will slacken, and you will slip into gathering mode. Listen to the chorus of the birds. Smell the essential odours of the forest, the blend of dark earth and delicate floral notes. Feel the soft, mossy carpet under your feet. Nibble on a wood sorrel leaf and feel your appetite instantly quicken. Then look down and turn all your attention to the lush forest floor in all its hundred shades of green: moss, lichen, bracken, and leaves. Bring your mushroom gaze into focus and gradually home in on the details. Is that another shade of green there? Is there something hiding under those dry, brown leaves, peeking shyly out at you?

Traces of life

We make choices as nations. We make choices as individuals. And all the choices we make leave a trace.

What sort of traces will we leave? Those of us who grew up in a former British colony read the poem *Ozymandias* at school. Written by Percy Bysshe Shelley in 1817, it was inspired by the Egyptian pharaoh, Ramesses II, also known as Ozymandias. Occasionally these lines from it come to mind:

> My name is Ozymandias, king of kings:
> Look on my works, ye Mighty, and despair!

These few words were all that was left on the pedestal of the shattered royal statue which lay 'half-sunk' in the sand. Glory and fame are transitory and even monuments built out of the hardest stone have a sad habit of crumbling with age. In the business world they talk about creating values. But the values we leave behind us when we die are of a very different order.

In Eiolf's case, it's not just the memory of the calibre of his relationships with his nearest and dearest that endures, but also of the bonds he formed with so many people far beyond kith and kin. At the funeral, a woman who worked in the canteen at

Eiolf's office wrote in the memorial book that he was one of the few people in the office who spoke to the 'canteen lady'. She thanked him for that. A full year after his death I was on a tour of a housing estate as part of a job I was working on. Although I didn't know it, this estate had been one of Eiolf's projects as an architect. Our guide spoke in glowing terms of his collaboration with the architect and mentioned Eiolf by name, unaware that his wife was actually present. A huge lump came into my throat when I heard this; I was totally unprepared for it. Architects have an advantage over the rest of us, in that they leave behind a solid, tangible legacy in their buildings. Structures which embody the architect's ideas, their designs; frozen in time and still perceptible long after the architect is gone. Eiolf's buildings embrace and comfort me every time I visit them.

The good name we leave behind us, our posthumous reputation, is not something that money can buy or that can be carved in stone for eternity. It is something we build up little by little, day in, day out, in our dealings with the people around us. Eiolf's generosity towards his fellow human beings made me the widow of a good man. It's always heartening to hear little stories of things he did or said. I'm still surprised by the number of lives he touched. This goes for children, too: Eiolf loved to sit and draw with them and draw pictures for them. Leave such values as these behind you and you live on after you are dead. I treasure these stories about Eiolf like rare emeralds.

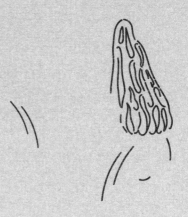

True morels:
the diamonds
of the fungi
kingdom

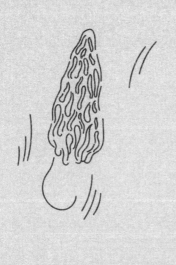

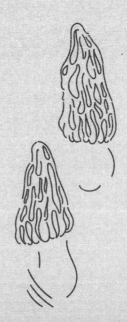

How could Eiolf just collapse and die? To begin with, that was all I could think of. Why didn't we know he was ill? What could we have done? What had the doctor missed? A man I knew offered to take a closer look at Eiolf's medical record. He was a specialist in the very condition that had taken Eiolf's life. My initial reaction was to accept his offer because I wanted to know as much as possible. No sooner had I said yes, however, than I went off the idea: more information wasn't going to change anything. To be presented with the knowledge of what we might have done differently at some point would only be upsetting. Eiolf was already dead.

The number one mushroom on my personal top five list is the true morel, *Morchella conica*. This particular mushroom does not look particularly appetising. It looks like a shrivelled brain on a stalk, but for a mushroom hunter there is no greater thrill than to lay hands on this great delicacy. The true morel is a member of the *Morchella* genus. The word 'morel' comes from the French *morille*, stemming from the Dutch *morilhe*, which in turn is related to Old High German *morhila*, a diminutive of *moraha*, meaning carrot. According to veterans of my local society in Oslo, finding true morels is a very rare occurrence. One elderly gentleman in his eighties told me that he had come across them only three times in his long mushrooming career. Many mushroom pickers have never found them and have had to content themselves with 'liking' other people's finds on social media.

For my own part, the only ones I had tasted had been purchased for an exorbitant sum of money. I had long wondered whether I would ever manage to find true morels in the wild.

Hunting for true morels in New York

My American friend R. keeps dried mushrooms in her larder. Every time I open the larder door I am struck by the rich, enticing scent of the true morels, even though they are safely stored in a sealed glass jar. It's an intense aroma, almost primitive, animal-like. Not so surprising, perhaps, for a mushroom which — according to Professor Gro Gulden, writing in the Norwegian Mycological Association's magazine, *Sopp og nyttevekster* (*Mushrooms and Useful Plants*) — came into existence 130 million years ago and lived in peaceful co-existence with the dinosaurs. It is a scent which can arouse a powerful longing even in those who have forgotten where it comes from. R. saves her true morels for special occasions. And until such an occasion comes along you are treated to this extra-terrestrial sensory experience every time you open the larder door.

A friend who is a chef says that the most expensive dish in his restaurant is steak with morels and that all the chefs have been given strict instructions to use no more than one true morel per steak. One half of the morel is chopped up and added to the sauce while the other is used as garnish. In other words, you don't have to use pounds and pounds of true morels to lend a true fillip to a dish. They may be expensive, but a small amount is all you need to lift a meal.

True morels appear in the spring, like a fanfare heralding Nature's return to life. I visited R. in New York in May, when the morels should normally be out. But the weather was still cold. The freshly opened pink flowers on the magnolia tree looked a mite chilly, as if they had bloomed a couple of weeks too soon. R. and I wrapped up well and drove out to what — after inquiring discreetly of those in the know — we believed to be the most promising morel spot on the Hudson River. Although we didn't say as much to one another on the drive there, I'm pretty certain we both cherished the same glimmer of hope: what if we found true morels in New York? Now that would be something to shout about. I could already picture the envy coming off fellow mushroomers in waves.

The forest floor was covered in old, brown leaves and thin, tough twigs. The air was damp, the spring leaves were a little slippery underfoot, and the paths we tramped along were rather muddy. There weren't many other people around so early in the day. The elusive woodland smells of unfamiliar trees and nuts filled the clear spring air. We were both very focused, neither of us saying a word. We could clearly see our car on the one side of the 'forest' and the rows of apartment buildings on the other. We could hear the city sounds of traffic, dogs, and dog owners, but there was no doubt that we were in a forest, an urban forest in the middle of New York. Even so, this was nothing like the experience of being in a Norwegian forest, where you can drink in the silence and savour the mingled scents of growth and decay from the forest floor. There civilisation can very quickly become a distant memory.

We had consulted books and the Internet to find out how an elm tree looks. In the United States — unlike in Norway — one is advised to look for true morels under elms. Langdon Cook, author of *The Mushroom Hunters*, mentions professional gatherers' experience of the relationship between true morels and elm trees. In *A Morel Hunter's Companion*, Nancy Smith Weber writes that elm trees are particularly important, but that beechwoods with a scattering of maple, elm, cherry, and ash are also classic hunting grounds for true morels. Smith Weber goes on to say that while dead elm trees are a tragedy for forests, parks, and streets, the morel hunter has a good chance of finding true morels near such lost trees. According to her, the Dutch elm disease which ravaged these trees in the state of Michigan also spelled the start of a real morel bonanza which lasted for several years. The link between morels and particular species of trees is branded on the minds of true morel hunters in America. In Norway, on the other hand, true morels are *not* generally associated with any particular trees as they are saprophytes and feed off dead organic matter. What is always interesting, when it comes to accepted truths about mushrooms in other countries, is the way in which they highlight our own preconceived notions.

After several hours of hunting we had to conclude, somewhat reluctantly, that the woods on the banks of the Hudson had no true morels to offer on that cold morning. The only thing we had gained from this expedition was that we had learned how to recognise the elm. Shivering slightly, and with our baskets empty of morels, we drove home. A cosy glow from the windows welcomed us back and it was good to walk in to a warm apartment after having braved the brisk spring weather in hope of making a dream of a find.

To cheer us up R. decided that the dried morels should be taken from the larder, prepared, and eaten, with a prayer for better luck next time. We spent the rest of the day drinking tea which warmed us inside and out, browsing through recipes, and planning our meal. And as we sat there, considering and assessing possible dishes, the conversation soon turned to earlier mushroom finds.

In America as in Norway, a blissful look comes over the faces of mushroom gatherers as they relive the highlights of their mushrooming career: setting, date, place, species — all are included in the retelling of historic discoveries from years, decades, earlier. Little tales and long yarns are spun around the mushroom and we have no trouble picturing the forest, the atmosphere, and the circumstances surrounding the great find.

A typical mushrooming high point is the discovery of a rare specimen. While some species are regarded as 'close to endangered', others are already 'regionally extinct'. If someone finds a rare mushroom that is also either seriously or critically endangered, word spreads very fast. Reports of sites where such finds have been made can prompt people to drive hundreds of miles just to see this wonder with their own eyes. One acquaintance of mine drove almost 400 miles to see the Spring Orange Peel Fungus, *Caloscypha fulgens*, *in situ*. As she herself summed up the experience later, smiling happily: 'It's not bad being a mushroom maniac.'

My own most spectacular find — a mushroom which aroused quite a lot of mycological interest — was made not in Norway, but in the United States. It happened on the last day of the Telluride Mushroom Festival. Gary Lincoff, with whom I had walked round New York's Central Park on a previous occasion, was reviewing all of the mushrooms found on that day's expedition. I was feeling a bit tired so I sat down on a large rock nearby. Glancing around I noticed two fairly large, white mushrooms in the grass. I picked them, thinking at first that they might be Penny Buns, but they were a little too white. When I showed the others my mushrooms Lincoff gave a great whoop and almost jumped up and down with excitement. It appeared that my find was a minor mycological event and I was talked into donating one of my mushrooms 'to science'. Fortunately

I was able to keep the smaller and nicer of the two. It seemed likely that what I had found was *Boletus barrowsii* or the White King Bolete. What was so special about this discovery was that this mushroom had never been found in Telluride before. It had been thought that the climate in Telluride was a little too harsh for it. But that was before *I* found it growing there.

'What's your surname?' I was asked by one of the scientific advisors. I eyed him uncertainly.

'If it turns out that what you've found is actually a new species it might be called after you,' he explained. Okay!

My find was remarkable enough to be mentioned in Lincoff's closing speech at the Festival. I was told that I would be informed of the results of the DNA test when these were forthcoming, probably in a few months' time. I still haven't heard anything, so I'm guessing that my addition to the knowledge of *Boletus barrowsii* is limited to the proof that it also grows in Telluride, Colorado, and that I had not contributed to science by discovering a new species.

It has sometimes seemed to me that the individual mushroom gatherer's rites of passage almost rival the other key events in their lives. The first time you find a true morel could be said to be just such an event; the moment when you join the select company of those who have found true morels in the wild.

R. and I eventually decided to make chicken with morel and cognac sauce:

Chicken with Morel and Cognac Sauce

Pre-heat the oven to 180°C (370°F).

Soak 40 grams of dried true morels in two tablespoons of cognac for 15 minutes, then drain, reserving the liquid.

Sauté the morels in a tablespoon of butter for 15 minutes. You can see soon see where this is going — and it's going to be good! Add 120 millilitres of single cream to the morels and simmer until the liquid has reduced by half. Sprinkle with half a teaspoon of salt and a pinch of cayenne pepper.

Now for the chicken (1½ kilograms will feed four people): rub a whole bird with a tablespoon of butter, salt, and pepper. Spoon the morels into the body cavity then roast the chicken with the breast side up for 20 minutes. Turn the chicken and roast it for another 20 minutes. Turn again and roast for 20 minutes breast side up again. The chicken is cooked through when the juices run clear. Another way of knowing when the chicken is done is to use a meat thermometer. When this reads 72°C, take the bird out of the oven, remove the morels from it, and leave it to rest.

Pour the juices from the roasting pan into a small saucepan, add 60 millilitres of white wine, the mushroomy cognac, the morels from inside the chicken, and 140 millilitres of single cream. Let all of this simmer for five minutes.

Cut the chicken into 8 pieces, arrange on a platter, and pour the morel sauce over them just before serving.

This is a sauce that seriously challenges good table manners, so great is the temptation to give in to slurping and finger-licking. The dried true morels were very good, but there's no doubt that it would have been even better if we had found them ourselves on the banks of the Hudson.

Morels are sac fungi, which is to say: they produce spores in a sac-like structure and not in the gills under the cap or elsewhere. As do subterranean truffles. This fact is only of interest to mush-roomers who categorise genera according to how the spores are spread and how a mushroom reproduces itself. Most people know of true morels and truffles because both are sought-after delicacies, as the prices they command will testify. The word 'truffle' comes from the French word *truffe*, possibly stemming from the Latin *tuber*, meaning a lump or swelling. Subterranean truffle tubers can be sniffed out by well-trained truffle pigs or truffle hounds. The exclusive white truffle can cost as much as £3,500 per pound, while the more common black truffle can be yours for around £1,300 per pound. If the black truffle is gastronomic gold then the white truffle is the diamond of the fungi world. And at these prices it's hardly surprising that a special tool, a razor-sharp slicer, is used to shave off wafer-thin slivers of truffle. According to one Norwegian chef all you need, to create pure culinary magic, is one third of an ounce of white truffle per head.

Dried true morels are much more reasonably priced. A pound of these will only set you back £170. Once you have tasted slow-fried true morels it's easy to understand why they are so expensive. The scent of true morels sizzling in a sauce of butter, sherry, and cream can very quickly bring people streaming to the kitchen from all over the house. After eating true morels for the first time, one friend dubbed them 'sweetmeats'. In any case, when you start measuring things in ounces rather than pounds it's fair to assume that you're dealing either with narcotics or rare mushrooms.

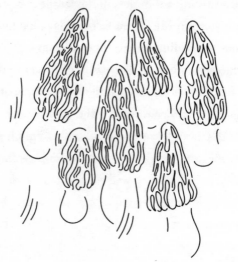

Morchella conica, true morels

In the United States, there are competitions and festivals devoted to true morels. Who will find the first or last one of the season? Who will find the most? Who is the year's national true morel champion? In the States they have electronic maps on which, each spring, you can follow the true morel's slow but sure arrival in a forest near you. For the state of Michigan, known for its true morels, the mushroom is an excellent money-spinner, attracting tourists at a time of year when not much else is going on. In New York, the New York Mycological Society organises a true morel expedition for its members each spring. Throughout the rest of the season, the Society arranges trips that are also open to non-members for a nominal fee. This principle does not extend, however, to the true morel expedition. Springtime's loveliest adventure for the New York Mycological Society is a members-only event. My friend R. has gone along on this trip several times. According to her, these outings usually yield no decent pickings to speak of. Normally they don't find anything at all. But they always finish up at the home of one of the members, who invites everyone back for a hot meal, so the social element makes up for the empty mushroom baskets, and it's a nice way of marking the start of the season.

The night I arrived in New York, I dreamed of Eiolf. We were at an old-fashioned amusement park with a bunch of friends. Something caught my eye, I glanced away for a moment, and when I turned back Eiolf wasn't there. A split-second and he was gone. We ran around the amusement park, looking for him and calling his name, but he was nowhere to be seen. We were frantic, frustrated, and yet it made me happy, that dream, like all the other dreams I've had about Eiolf. It was almost as if he had dropped by to say hello. The fact that he had looked in while I was in New York made our friends there happy too. Eiolf was dead, but in social terms he was still alive. In some strange way our friends felt that he was there with us. He's not here with me, but he's not gone either. I always find him somewhere, even in New York.

Hipster morels

The true morel is a master of disguise. In its various shades of beige, brown, grey, and black it doesn't exactly cry out to be found in a bone-dry, wintry landscape, among all the dead twigs, moss, grass, and leaves of similar hues. If you walk along the foot of a hillside and look up, in the right light it can be easier to spot the silhouette of a mushroom. If you find one, stop and inspect the area round about — true morels tend to grow close together. It's also a good idea to take a closer look at seemingly uninteresting dead leaves, since true morels can often be found peeping out between them. In fact it really is just a matter of following the same procedure as always when hunting for mushrooms, but with an even keener mushroom eye.

When garden centres started importing bark for use as ground cover in flower beds they also transformed the growing conditions for true morels. True morels can now be found among the bark chips in private gardens, in public parks, on the central reservations of dual carriageways, and even on ski-jump hills and ski slopes. Which is not to say that true morels are springing up all over the place, but the chances of finding them are certainly better now.

I know it's silly to ascribe human qualities to mushrooms, but it's hard not to feel that mushrooms in general, and the elusive morel in particular, are playing hide-and-seek with us. Not just once, but time and again, after spending half a day hunting for a particular mushroom in the forest, we have found it right next to the car. I can almost hear the mushroom chuckling to itself when we finally meet. From its point of view we obviously haven't looked hard enough or been smart enough.

It's easy to become superstitious. There are so many variables to be considered when out mushroom hunting. I have seen otherwise rational individuals deliberately selecting the smallest basket from the back seat of the car when going foraging, not wanting to push their mushrooming luck. Sometimes they don't take a basket with them at all — hoping that the less well-prepared they are, the luckier they will be. If you have ever come upon a whole swathe of a sought-after mushroom, stretching as far as the eye can see, and had no basket to hand, it's easy to become superstitious yourself.

I had to wait some years before finding my first true morels. I remember how I pricked up my ears when my friend K. told me that he had stumbled upon some true morels in a flower bed on the east side of Oslo. Urban mushrooms in the hipster heartland of Grünerløkka! He hadn't picked them though, because he felt they were 'a little too exposed' to the dirt and dust and fumes of the city.

'Well,' I said, 'when it comes to true morels I have no such reservations.'

I may have spoken a little too soon and sounded a little too eager, although I did try to act as though I was only mildly interested. Inside me morel chaos reigned, with all sorts of feelings jostling for position.

'Would you like to go and have a look?' he asked. Now there was an offer I couldn't refuse.

In my rucksack I had some newly purchased asparagus. For the true gourmet, morels and asparagus is the springtime dish to beat all springtime dishes. So, as good luck would have it, I was all set to go true morel hunting with K. right then and there.

K. took me to the spot. At first I saw nothing of interest. You really have to bring your true morel gaze into sharp focus. I didn't see the morels until K. pointed to a spot in the grass. And there they were. Wow! I didn't know whether to shout out loud or clap my hand over my mouth and utter a silent Munch-like scream. If there is one mushroom that could be described as glamorous it has to be the true morel. It was one of those stellar moments granted to very few mushroom pickers. This was how I was presented with my own secret true morel site in the heart of the Norwegian capital.

The Brain Mushroom:
the black sheep of the mushroom family

There are true morels and then there are the false sort. False morels are not a species, but an umbrella term covering several species belonging to the *Gyromitra, Helvella,* and *Verpa* genera. The course for the mushroom inspector's exam also covers the notorious Brain Mushroom, *Gyromitra esculenta,* categorised on the List of Standards as 'highly toxic'. While true morels are rare, Brain Mushrooms are fairly common, particularly alongside bark-strewn, floodlit ski-trails. On the mushroom for beginners course we were taught that the mycotoxins in the Brain Mushroom may cause sterility and that it contains a component also found in rocket fuel. This last fact always makes a big impression on people new to the course, hearing it for the first time. The mycotoxin in the Brain Mushroom is also reputed to be carcinogenic. On the course we learned that the toxin in the Brain Mushroom is activated by poisonous metabolites which attack the nervous system. According to the health authorities, the ingestion of a small amount of this spring mushroom can lead to 'a general feeling of unwellness and headaches' after five to eight hours. Ingestion of larger amounts could cause damage to the liver, kidneys, and red blood cells. Not exactly something you'd want to eat, you might think.

As a newcomer to the mushroom community I found it rather strange, therefore, the way in which some older mushroomers could be rather evasive when the subject of Brain Mushrooms came up. I had the feeling that they were holding something back.

Were they not telling the whole truth? Were they hiding something? Had I caught a sly look there or not?

If you happen to find an old mushroom guide in a

second-hand bookshop or on a dusty shelf in a holiday cottage you will notice the two crosses *and* the three stars given alongside the Brain Mushroom. As we know, two crosses means 'highly toxic' and three stars means 'very tasty'. Between the crosses and the stars is a small circle, meaning 'after preparation'. So, according to some old mushroom guides, the Brain Mushroom is a highly toxic mushroom, but one which can be very tasty when well cooked. Perhaps that explains the epithet *esculenta*, which is Latin for 'edible'.

A friend who is a chef told me how, in the old days, he used to cook Brain Mushrooms and serve them to guests in his restaurant. This was before 1963, the year when the Brain Mushroom was redefined as 'highly toxic' rather than 'edible' in Norway. This recategorisation was prompted by a number of deaths recorded elsewhere in the world, albeit due to the consumption of improperly prepared Brain Mushrooms.

I made a few discreet enquiries. 'What would proper preparation of Brain Mushrooms entail?' I asked. This was a touchy subject, that much I had gathered. It turned out that it was also one which elicited widely diverse opinions — and strong feelings.

I'd never heard of what is known as mushroom detoxification before so I was all ears. Everyone who had 'detoxified' mushrooms agreed that they had to be blanched. The toxin gyromitrin is volatile and water soluble. The blanching ought preferably to be done outside, but if you have to do this dirty job indoors be sure to have the cooker hood turned full on. I received rather conflicting information on how long the blanching should take and how many times it should be repeated. But all were agreed that it had to be done more than once and that the water obviously could not be used for a sauce or a stew, but had to be thrown away. It seemed like an awful lot of bother to me. And the blanching was just the start, because the Brain Mushrooms then had to be dried and stored, preferably for weeks, months, or years: opinions also varied on how long one ought to wait before eating them. In any case, you know you're dealing with genuine mushroom nerds when you have individuals who are willing to follow this elaborate process of preparation — which they *hope* will remove the poison, or most of it at any rate. How much one can eat of these controversial mushrooms, how often, and over how long a period of time, is an obscure science fraught with potential pitfalls. For the record, it should be said that I have also heard stories of people who have eaten and enjoyed Brain Mushrooms for years only to suddenly fall ill. It is almost as if the poison builds up in the system until the day when the body says enough is enough. That is a risk run by everyone who defies the List of Standards and chooses to eat Brain Mushrooms.

The edibility of the Brain Mushroom can also give rise to fierce debate on social media, especially if there are Scandinavians involved. To anyone new to the mushroom community, the vehemence and uncompromising nature of these heated exchanges might seem quite shocking. The question as to whether the Brain Mushroom can be eaten or not provokes strong emotions in normally mild-mannered citizens. While this mushroom is officially designated as highly toxic in Norway it can be bought quite openly just across the border in Sweden and ordered in upmarket Swedish restaurants. In Finland no one has any qualms about eating what they consider 'delicious' Brain Mushrooms. I once received a present from Finland: a jar of dried Brain Mushrooms, duly and correctly prepared. I have to admit that this gift is still sitting, untouched, in my kitchen cupboard. But one thing, at least, is clear: if a certified mushroom expert is presented with Brain Mushrooms at an inspection checkpoint every last one will be given the thumbs-down.

What the experts do at inspection checkpoints is one thing, what some of those same experts eat when they're not wearing their inspector hats is, however, an entirely different matter.

One year, on 17 May, Norway's Constitution Day, I received proof that even those generally regarded as the strictest guardians of the List of Standards eat Brain Mushrooms themselves — after proper and painstaking preparation, of course. After a sumptuous Constitution Day lunch it was time for some exercise. Time to go Brain Mushroom hunting! So no embroidered national costumes — the traditional 17 May garb — for these keen Brain Mushroom foragers. Here warm outdoor clothing was the order of the day. Everyone was looking forward to having Brain Mushrooms in port sauce for supper. Constitution Day celebrations can easily carry on late into the evening for those given to hunting and eating Brain Mushrooms.

'We're so old that it doesn't matter anyway,' one member of the group declared cheerfully.

'Personally, I would never give them to young people in their reproductive years,' another remarked, possibly wanting to reassure me that they weren't doing anything wrong.

'We only eat them on 17 May, just that one time in the year,' a third informed me, with a big smile.

I could scarcely believe my ears.

This simply supports the fundamental anthropological observation that people don't always practice what they preach. I was rather shocked, mainly perhaps because I had not expected experts like these to take such a calculated risk and actually eat Brain Mushrooms in their private lives. I suppose they could be compared to driving instructors breaking the speed limit when they are at the wheel, with no pupil in the car. To me, the certified mushroom professionals were like demi-gods — I looked up to them — but that day I discovered that they, too, were mere mortals.

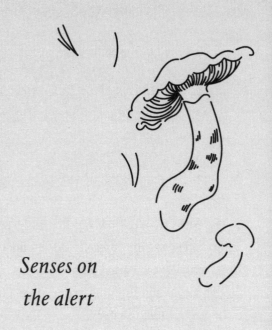

*Senses on
the alert*

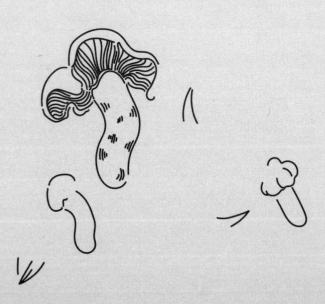

The paths were narrow and dry. My new acquaintance B. and I had wandered this way and that without really knowing where we were going. Behind us we left a little cloud of dust, like in cowboy films: a bad sign if it's not Indians but mushrooms you're after. The sunlight was bright, harsh. Had there been no rain here on the island earlier in the day, when it had rained on the mainland? Neither of us knew where best to start looking. While B. had cranked the handle on the cable ferry to carry us across the narrow strait, we had got talking to some cheery islanders who eyed our empty, but hopeful mushroom baskets curiously. No, nobody had ever found mushrooms on the island, we were told. But we chose to carry on, not to be put off by doubtful natives.

Suddenly, an opening appeared, leading into a dim, mysterious looking grove. Should we go that way? The forest path was bare and stony and yet I had the feeling that it could, nonetheless, be promising. The forest floor might have retained some of the moisture from the recent rainfall. In any case, it was good to get out of the sun and into the grove's shady embrace. It took a while for our eyes to adjust to the cool woodland light. We were bathed in a dancing, dappled patchwork of sunlight and shade and it would have been easy to give in to the temptation to just potter about, but I was on a mission, so I began to scan the terrain.

It wasn't long before my newly trained eye fell on a mushroom — the Miller Mushroom, *Clitopilus prunulus*, with which I had only just become fully *au fait*. A delicacy. I could almost hear my teacher's voice: lead-white caps, decurrent gills which can be pink-tinged, and, not least, a rather mealy odour. A truly yummy mushroom with some nasty lookalikes, so you really have to know how to tell the one from the other. And in this forest we found whole colonies of Miller Mushrooms. I picked a lovely specimen and handed it to B..

'Smell this!' I said brightly, turning the mushroom upside down and presenting the pale underside to him. He straightened up and took a big sniff of the gills. Then he went quiet.

'What do you smell?' I asked eagerly and a mite impatiently. I was keen to know whether B. could detect the odour of wet flour.

But: 'I'd rather not say,' he said, going rather pink. He didn't seem to know where to look or what to do with the mushroom.

A few long, quiet minutes went by. B. is red-haired and pale-skinned and it was hard for him to hide the fact that he was blushing. Oh, dear. I had put us both in a rather awkward situation. There I was, thinking that the answer would be easy and obvious and possibly help to stimulate a dawning interest in mushrooms. I had donned my cunning mushroom evangelist hat that day. The plan had been not to force fungi on him, but to let him discover them for himself as they showed up along our way.

We didn't know each other well enough for him to feel comfortable about telling me what the mushroom had actually smelled like to him and I didn't delve any deeper. I had no wish to render the situation even more awkward. But whatever it was it certainly wasn't wet flour.

All senses go

On the mushrooms for beginners course our teacher had told us that the surest way to determine whether a Russula mushroom is edible or not is to taste it. This presupposes, of course, that you know how to identify Russula mushrooms. One simple clue is that the stipe, or stem, of a Russula mushroom is brittle, unlike the stems of other mushrooms, which are fibrous. Once you are absolutely certain that what you have in your hand is a member of the Russula family you can take a tiny bite and roll it around your tongue. If it has a sharp, acrid taste, it is inedible and probably mildly toxic, while all mild tasting Russula are edible. No matter how they taste, all test bites should be spat out. This was an exercise which several members of the class, myself included, baulked at. We had just been told, after all, never to eat raw mushrooms. Nonetheless, the whole class was soon having a go, probably because we could see that the teacher had tasted Russulas and lived to tell the tale. The taste of an acrid Russula is one you soon learn to recognise. It's like chilli, horseradish, or wasabi: fiery, pungent, and instantly filling the mouth with a burning sensation.

Consistency and texture are also key factors when it comes to identifying mushrooms. Mushroom caps can be soft as velvet, tough and rubbery, smooth, coarse, dry, or sticky and plastered with dirt and grit and pine needles. The stems may be stubby and solid, slender and hollow, smooth, hairy, powdery, or *floc-cose*. *Flocci* are short, hair-like tufts. I gradually discovered that mycology has its own vocabulary for describing the parts of a mushroom. In my notebook from the beginners' course I made a note of the fact that the edible Ink Cap, usually found in gardens and parks, has flocci on the stem.

Since then I have learned that stems can be floccose or so 'loose' that they flake off onto the fingers when touched. Like brushing against wet paint. The Prince mushroom is a perfect example of this. According to those inclined to exaggerate, on some fungi the flocculence is so thick you could spread it with a knife, like soft cream cheese. Stems can also be reticulated, covered in a mesh-like pattern. The summer cep derives its Latin name, *Boletus reticulatus*, from its reticulated stipe. If I was to become fully conversant with this new subject I was also going to have to learn all this gobbledygook, which the more experienced mushroomers bandied about with the greatest of ease. The challenge seemed a formidable one.

Strange as it may seem, you can also use your ears to identify mushrooms. How does the song of the mushroom sound, a poet might wonder. Do mushrooms make a noise, others might ask. These questions call to mind the Zen *koan*: What is the sound of one hand clapping? The Peppery Bolete, *Chalciporus piperatus*, with its distinctive reddish pore surface, has a yellow stem of between 4 and 6 centimetres long which makes a faint popping sound when snapped, like a mycological champagne cork. If you want to hear a mushroom sing you simply have to use your ears.

Our olfactory sense is central to our experience of eating and tasting food. Researchers estimate that the perception of flavours is 75–95 per cent dependent on smell. Without smell, coffee would be nothing but black, bitter water — a weird thought to most coffee drinkers, including me, who had started drinking coffee after Eiolf died. If we lose our sense of smell — when we have a cold, for example — food tastes of 'nothing', or rather, we register only one of the five basic tastes: salt, sweet, bitter, sour, or umami. Umami, what's that, some might ask. Umami is a relatively new word to the English language, first used around 1979. It is defined by experts as the taste of fermented protein — which doesn't leave us that much the wiser, but think of a good mature cheese, air-dried meat, bouillon, dehydrated seaweed, or mushrooms. The longer such foods are left to dry, cure, or ferment, the more intense the umami taste. Umami is the satisfying, long-lasting, smooth, rounded, sensual, complex flavour we find in cheese or cured meats. It makes them so more-ish. Research has shown that when two umami-rich ingredients are combined the end result is a regular umami bomb: in this case one plus one equals three. I discovered this for myself when I was invited to a smart dinner party at which we were served a delicious starter of preserved mushrooms: Penny Buns; Winter Mushrooms, *Flammulina velutipes*;

and shiitake, *Lentinus edodes*, in a herb marinade, sprinkled with grated *Västerbotten* cheese. *Västerbotten* cheese is the Swedish equivalent of parmesan and has a strong and complex flavour. This elegant starter represented a wonderful combination of Eastern and Western umami. The simplest way to give a dish some added pizzazz is to add some umami. A dash of umami can work magic, totally transforming yesterday's leftovers. And if you're looking for instant umami there is nothing quite like dried mushrooms.

Although all of the senses must be brought to bear in determining which species a mushroom belongs to, smell has a special part to play. The teacher on the mushrooms for beginners course showed us how to smell a mushroom. I found it odd, the way he stuck his nose right up against the under-side of the cap and inhaled deeply. Was it really necessary — or sensible — to breathe in mushroom spores in that way? Didn't one risk drawing the microscopic spores down into the lungs? The spores are spread by the wind and if they land in a spot where conditions are good they can produce new mushrooms. Fungi sprouting in the lungs didn't sound too great a prospect, though. The mushrooms were passed round the class in what I would learn was a standard teaching method, and everyone else sniffed away without hesitation. Apparently I was the only one with any reservations.

Nonetheless, I knuckled down to the task, smelled all the mushrooms, and did my best to sniff out the differences between them. My attempts to describe the various odours were less successful, however. Our perception of olfactory sensations is concrete and physical, but the language we use to describe them tends to be more abstract. We say: 'It smells like ...' The teachers on the course kept coming out with certain words: 'apricot', 'potato', 'flower', 'damp cloth', 'cellars', 'flea market', 'radish', and so on. The unique, pronounced odour of certain mushrooms is almost like a fingerprint, an infallible means of establishing their identity. Our teacher believed the aromas of some fungi were so distinctive that they could be identified blindfold. That sounded a bit like a circus act to me.

As a beginner I was confronted with a spectrum of aromas that I would never have associated with mushrooms. Anyone who has smelled the almondy scent of the Prince mushroom will find it hard to forget. Likewise, though for very different reasons, no one who has smelled the Common Stinkhorn's sweetish reek of rotting cadaver is likely to forget that in a hurry.

Our teacher told us that one important difference between, for example, the chanterelle and the false chanterelle, *Hygrophoropsis aurantiaca*, is their smell. The false chanterelle has no odour, unlike the chanterelle which, according to experts, smells of apricots. I've sniffed a lot of chanterelles and only with the greatest goodwill could I subscribe — still somewhat reluctantly — to that theory. And as a keen, if inexperienced, mushroom enthusiast, one does so want to show goodwill. But does the chanterelle smell of apricots because I *actually* smell apricots? Or do I think it smells of apricots because experienced mushroomers and fat mushroom guides tell me it does?

The balance of power between the aspirant and the mushroom professional is an unequal one. Factor in the psychology of expectations and the mushroom student doesn't stand a chance. And so she imagines she smells what those with more expertise say she should smell. Phantosmia is the term for imagined odours or olfactory hallucinations. This was a new word to me and one that was to prove very relevant. There's no doubt that I smell *something* when I sniff a chanterelle, but what?

This question of odour bothered me. I found it much easier to describe how a mushroom looked than how it smelled. I had read that while our visual sense is 'synthetic', our olfactory sense is 'analytical'. This means that if a red light and a green light are shone into the eye at the same time the eye will automatically read these two overlapping signals as 'yellow'. When we smell something, the process is quite different. The nose registers all the many components of the smell. The overall impression is, therefore, of a mosaic of individual scents. This blend of separate olfactory perceptions is analysed and compared to the archive of scents stored in the brain. Usually we do not have one word to cover this composite aroma. I had something approaching an 'Aha!' moment when I read this; I actually felt a little light-headed. Was I getting to the nub of the problem?

Further googling on smells reveals that individual olfactory perceptions vary much more than visual perceptions. Fluctuations in our health or mood can affect our sense of smell. And among people of the same age there will be some whose olfactory perception is 10 to 40 times weaker than that of their contemporaries. Olfactory sensitivity can also vary from substance to substance. That is to say, we can be 'blind' to certain smells, but not to others. One well known example is 'asparagus pee': after eating asparagus some people catch a whiff of sulphur or petrol, and/or a metallic odour in their urine, while others don't smell anything at all. Mycologist Michael Kuo of *Mushroomexpert. com* has described how he finds it hard to detect the 'phenolic', or carbolic, odour in some mushrooms, but is so sensitive to the 'farinaceous', or mealy, odour of other species that he can smell them from yards away. This, too, I found thought-provoking. Was my own sense of smell generally poorer than that of others, or were the problems I was having with detecting mushroom odours due to my general grief-stricken state?

We tend to associate certain people with how they smell. There is a possibly apocryphal story of how, after a successful campaign, Napoleon sent a note to his mistress, saying: 'Don't wash. I'm on my way home!' Smells reinforce our images of the people around us, negatively or positively. It's difficult to describe the odours of people we know, far easier to attach certain scents to them. Think of the powerful memories that can be triggered by smells from the past, that sensation of instantly being transported back in time. A friend whose father has been dead for over 40 years still uses his dad's desk every day. The interesting thing is, though, that he has never cleared out the desk drawers. He told me once that every now and again, when he opens a drawer, he can still smell his father. The desk is almost like a time capsule, taking him back to when his father was alive.

I envied him this and felt sad that I didn't have a drawer like that, full of Eiolf's things, that I could open and conjure up the smell of him. The only thing I can think of that has this effect is MacBaren's Amphora pipe tobacco. Its blend of cocoa and chocolate notes always takes me back to Eiolf's student days, when he smoked a pipe.

How do mushroom gatherers describe mushroom odours? More recent mushroom guides provide brief, simple descriptions, but in earlier literature we find fuller accounts. In an old Danish guide to mushrooms it says of the Overflowing Slimy Stem, *Limacella illinita*: 'Odour faint, first mealy or vaguely earthy, with an overtone of menthol or turpentine. Thereto, unpleasant suggestions of overripe meat, hen runs, wet dog, sweat, dirty laundry, or even unwashed public lavatories.'

In Norwegian books on mushrooms and fungi it is also not unusual to find mushroom odours described in terms such as 'pleasant' or 'unpleasant', which seems strange when one considers that smell, like taste, is highly subjective. For instance, one of my female mushroom buddies likes the smell of the Wood Blewit, *Lepista nuda*. Some mushroomers have described the odour of the Blewit as sweetish and simple. I don't like this mushroom, I think it smells of burnt rubber. My first teacher described the Blewit mushroom's odour as 'cod liver oil in Wellingtons'.

I was very happy, therefore, to read of the simple smell experiment carried out in Denmark, in the 1980s, by Poul Printz. Printz wrapped different species of mushroom separately in paper and asked people to sniff them. First, participants were asked to say whether they thought a smell was good or bad. Then they were asked to describe the smell. For the experiment Printz used mushrooms which were not widely known, to save the participants' learned expectations influencing their responses. The results of this experiment, which he describes in the journal of the Danish Society for the Promotion of Mushroom Knowledge, are very telling.

The article doesn't say how many people took part in the experiment, which ran for several years. Nonetheless, the conclusion has to be that olfactory preferences vary widely; the same mushroom can evoke diametrically opposite reactions from different people.

An obvious problem with subjective descriptions is that an individual's sense of smell also varies depending on their age, on whether they are taking particular medicines, and, for women, whether they are pregnant. The most experienced mushroom gatherers also talk of how their sense of smell improves in the course of the mushroom season. Some say their nose seems almost to go into hibernation in the winter months, gradually growing more sensitive as the frequency and pace of their mushrooming activities increases.

Mushroom	Individual participants' impression of smell	Description
Hebeloma radicosum Rooting Poison Pie	Good 75% Bad 25%	Marzipan, almonds, mothballs, chocolate cake, Nescafé
Inocybe hirtella Almond Fibrecap	Good 75% Bad 25%	Almond essence, radish, marzipan
Cortinarius rheubarbarinus (No common English name)	Good 50% Bad 50%	Radish, gas-like with overtones of cloves, pear, fresh sweetness
Russula foetens Stinking Russula	Good 40% Bad 40% Odourless 20%	Sweetish, honey, melon, strawberry, swimming pools, chlorine, almonds, wet blackboard sponge
Cortinarius traganus Gassy Webcap	Good 20% Bad 70% Neutral 10%	Soap, metallic, rubber, fruity, bad breath, plum compôte

The perception of smells is not only subjective, it is also culturally dictated. As a nation we are socialised to like certain smells more than others. A look at the list of the ten bestselling perfumes in different countries reveals clear variations in what is deemed to be the best fragrance. Chanel No. 5 is number one in France (and has been for years), but has never topped the chart in the United States. A smell expert who I spoke to told me that culture plays a large part in determining which scents we favour: the Germans like pine, the French prefer floral scents, the Japanese go for delicate fragrances, while North Americans are fond of what he described as 'bold smells', such as 'clear pine notes'.

These national differences are also reflected in the cuisine of individual countries. On the menu in Iceland you will find buried, rotten, fermented shark and manure-smoked mutton — for which sheep manure is mixed with straw and used to smoke salted mutton — and in Norway they have their own rotten fish delicacy, *rakfisk*, trout or char which is salted and fermented for anything from a few months to a full year, then eaten uncooked. Where the natives of some countries smell manure, others smell only sweet perfume and the promise of a wonderful meal. Variations in national preferences as regards mushroom aromas come as no surprise, therefore: the Clouded Agaric, *Clitocybe nebularis*, is described by Norwegian experts as 'perfumed' and is considered to be edible after decocting. Americans, on the other hand, never touch it, claiming that it smells 'skunky'.

The best example of differing national penchants for particular odours is the furore surrounding *Tricholoma matsutake*, the Matsutake or Pine Mushroom. The Matsutake is one of the most expensive mushrooms on the market, its price increasing year on year as it becomes ever more scarce in Japan. This species was first scientifically described in 1905, on the basis of a find made by the Norwegian Axel Blytt in the hills above Oslo. Blytt must have found the smell of this mushroom revolting since he gave it the epithet *nauseosa*. The famous American mycologist, David Arora, was less harsh in his judgement. In his opinion the

Matsutake smells of 'dirty socks'. The Japanese are of an entirely different opinion. In 1925, the Japanese researchers S. Ito and S. Imai described the mushroom and dubbed it *Matsutake*, the Japanese word for 'Pine Mushroom'. According to them it smells 'divine', an impression echoed by the old Japanese saying, 'For fragrance, choose Matsutake'. In 1999 it was established, in an almost thriller-like dénouement, that *Tricholoma matsutake* in Japan and *Tricholoma nauseosum* in Norway were one and the same species. According to scientific custom and the rules of nomenclature the first person to describe the mushroom gets to name it. Tradition would dictate, therefore, that this species ought to be called *Trichonoma nauseosum*.

The Japanese weren't happy about that at all. In Japan they wear cotton gloves to pick Matsutakes, to save the sebum on their fingers from sullying the mushrooms' perfection. Matsutakes have always been used by the Japanese as gifts of the first water, exchanged at solemn ceremonies, and poems were written about this mushroom's great virtues as far back as 759 BC. In the 12th century women at the Japanese court — always very much a man's world — were actually forbidden to say the word 'Matsutake', which also happens to be a slang word for penis. In the case of the mushroom, however, it is not size that matters, but how young and plump and proud it is. In modern-day Japan the market for Matsutake is nigh on insatiable. This is partly due to the belief that it has a Viagra-like effect on men. It was almost an insult to the honour of the Japanese nation for their precious Matsutake to be given such an ugly sounding scientific name. How could their national treasure be stuck for ever with the name 'nauseating mushroom'? Japanese lobbyists mounted a massive PR campaign and eventually won the right for the mushroom to be called *T. matsutake*.

Tricholoma matsutake, Pine Mushroom

When a group of Norwegian mushroomers whom I know found some *T. matsutake* on their own home soil they decided it was finally time to try cooking them. They fried them in the usual Norwegian manner, with butter, salt, and pepper. But the result was not to their liking. At first I thought this must have had something to do with the Norwegian palate, but later I came across the following explanation: mushrooms with an aroma that is fat-soluble are best cooked with butter. The Matsutake's aroma is water-soluble, so this mushroom only really comes into its own when used in soup or with rice. To make Matsutake rice Japanese style, bring the rice to the boil, add a handful of chopped Matsutakes, turn down the heat, and cover with a lid. Then it's simply a matter of waiting for the flavours of the rice and the mushrooms to blend and harmonise. This method is supposed to raise the rice to undreamt-of heights. According to the Japanese, at any rate.

Another reason the mushrooming community needs to do more research into the olfactory aspect is that some of the standard terms used to describe mushroom aromas refer to things of which almost no one today has any practical knowledge. Take the Goatcheese Webcap, *Cortinarius camphoratus*, for instance. According to Norwegian mushroom guides it smells of burnt horn, goat barns, or rutting billy-goats. It's debatable how helpful such references are to most people, in Norway or elsewhere, unless they happen to have spent a lot of wintry hours in a goat barn and witnessed the dehorning of two-day old kids. To someone like myself, born in a small town — which is to say a town the size of a Norwegian city — in Malaysia, such a description certainly means very little. Another good example is the Goat Moth Wax Cap, *Hygrophorus cossus*. This reportedly smells of goat moth larvae, which burrow into the trunks of willow trees. Although goat moth larvae do have a quite distinct odour it's unlikely that many people, apart from entomologists, would be able to identify it. And anyway, who wants to smell a big, fat, scarlet larva with fearsome jaws. Or what about the *Hygrocybe foetens*, said to smell of mothballs, and the Tawny Webcap,

Cortinarius callisteus, which apparently smells of railway engines? And how many people would recognise the phenolic odour which is supposed to be a vital clue to identifying the poisonous *Agaricus* species?

The scent of apricots and other (learned?) aromas

My attempts to familiarise myself with the smell of chanterelles have led me to the conclusion that the generally accepted descriptions of mushroom odours are often used as abbreviations for a much wider olfactory landscape. The terminology employed in mushroom guides seems to me to be somewhat lacking. *Everything* one smells when one sniffs a mushroom is often reduced to one standard descriptor. Leading lights in the community remind us again and again that there are no shortcuts where mushrooms are concerned, although this is what all beginners pray for. But, when it comes to defining how mushrooms smell, plenty of shortcuts seem to be taken, even by leading experts in the field. The Horse Mushroom, *Agaricus arvensis*, smells of almonds, they say. The Tawny Milk Cap, *Lactarius volemus*, smells of shellfish. The Grey Veiled Amanita, *Amanita porphyria*, smells of raw potato. And so on and so forth. Wine experts and beer experts have developed a whole vocabulary to describe and capture the multi-faceted aromascape they encounter when they raise a glass of wine or beer to their noses, but mushroom experts seem to do the exact opposite, *reducing* the olfactory complexity with their limited range of descriptors. I suspect that this is not so much because mushroom aromas are all that different from those of wine or beer, but more because the mushroom community is stuck down a side road in the olfactory landscape.

The challenge for the beginner is to figure out what mushroomers actually mean when they speak of 'almonds', 'shellfish' or 'raw potato'. Experienced mushroom gatherers know how the Crab Brittlegill, *Russula xerampelina*, smells: of Crab Brittlegill, of course. And so seasoned hands become lost in tautological labyrinths. Mycocentrics, the insiders of the mushroom world, have forgotten what it's like to have to familiarise oneself with the smell of the Crab Brittlegill, and have few tips to offer the beginner, who stands on the outside, wanting to come in. The challenge for this beginner was to get the standard terminology to tally with the aromascape that met my nose on contact with the mushroom.

Much later, after I had become a certified mushroom inspector, I took a group on a trip to the island of Hovedøya in Oslo Fjord to pick St George's mushrooms. There were a few beginners in the party who had never seen the St George's before. We found the first specimens almost as soon as we arrived on the island. It's always fun to see people who aren't all that familiar with the world of mycology experience the joy of mushrooming for the first time. It's not only their eyes that light up, but every part of them. They smile, they giggle, they laugh out loud. The more demonstrative among them whoop, jump up and down, and wave their arms in the air. Then, as guide, I will often point them in the direction of other mushrooms, simply to have the pleasure of their grateful bows again. They find it hard to believe that anyone would want to share their mushroom discoveries with them. They've all heard about the secretiveness of the mushroom community, but I have an ulterior motive for being so generous. I have a specific question for them: What does the St George's mushroom smell of?

Everyone agrees that this mushroom has a distinctive odour, one not normally associated with mushrooms. I received a wide variety of answers: varnish, fresh paint, creosote, petrol, rancid oil, walnut, and even naphthalene, the main ingredient in mothballs. One person even thought it smelled 'fermented'.

I noted with interest that no one described it as 'mealy' or mentioned wet flour, the standard field guide description. Later that same day I happened to run into a famous chef who told me in glowing terms of making a big St George's find on Bygdøy. He had known this mushroom as a child, but had not come across it again until that moment. He had recognised it right away though, partly due to its smell. Without any prompting from me he launched into a long rant against the constant reference in field guides to wet flour as the St George's official odour. Unlike most people, he had approached the question methodically. He sprinkled flour with water, sniffed it, and then sniffed the mushroom. He came to the conclusion that the St George's does *not* smell of wet flour. He may be right about this. Dane Poul Printz says that to writers of an earlier age the smell of wet flour was 'the far more pungent stench of old flour lying in caked clumps in the kneading trough or left in the flour store from last year's harvest'. In other words, the references in the guides to a floury or mealy odour may be the scent of a bygone day when flour was not sold in pristine paper bags in the supermarket, a scent that most of us have never known.

I recently took another group of absolute beginners on a trip, the sole purpose of which was to introduce them to a couple of edible mushrooms and a few of the main toxic species. One of the first mushrooms we found was the Goatcheese Webcap, notorious in mushrooming circles for its awful smell. I split the mushroom down the middle and got everyone in the group to smell it. To my surprise opinions were divided: half of them thought it smelled disgusting, the others found its odour 'nice and perfumy'. Since then I've repeated this exercise with every new group of beginners, who haven't yet been socialised to the standard descriptors of the mushroom world. Always with the same result. This small example can perhaps serve as further proof that there is no point in trying to describe a mushroom's aroma from a subjective standpoint. And that as far as the Goatcheese Webcap is concerned, it might be that mushroomers think it smells bad because they have *learned* that it does.

I understand the instinct to cling to the standard answers when you find yourself in unknown territory, whether as a new traveller in the fungi kingdom or a widow new to the realms of grief. Unfortunately, the lines thrown to me are not always the most helpful.

I find the everyday euphemisms for death exasperating. Are they meant to smooth over the situation? Why can't people just call a spade a spade? I'm hyper-sensitive, almost everything gets on my nerves, both what is said and what is left unsaid. Some people are too nosy and pushy, while others remain strangely distant. People who are afraid of saying something wrong or of rubbing salt in the wound have the least to offer. There is no solace to be had from people who act as if nothing has happened, who avoid the subject or are simply conspicuous by their absence, only disappointment and resignation. Are they doing it for my sake or their own? It's even worse when they think of themselves as good friends. I haven't the strength to make allowances. I act and react with no thought for whether I'm creating a bad atmosphere or upsetting others. I'm not in full control of what I say or do and don't know who, when or how I'm offending. I've grown short-sighted and can see nothing but my own grief.

Normally, those of us who are cast out onto the seas of grief are given only platitudes to steer by. Well-meaning advice to get a dog, or clumsy reassurances that I was still young and would find someone else were of no help. If I'd had more energy they would have infuriated me. In terms of guidance, most advice — given with the best will in the world — was totally useless. To look ahead, to draw a line, and not look back — that didn't work for me. Most people seem to think that life's misfortunes should be put behind us as quickly as possible and that you simply have to grit your teeth and get on with it. I don't have much time for this strategy. If you ask me, all it does is cause grief to the poor teeth. In my experience, the ability of platitudes to give comfort is close to zero, but because even I don't know how best to dull the pain it's hard for me to ask for exactly what I need. When words of comfort are useless we — both those who need comfort and those try- ing to comfort — are doubly helpless.

As a relatively young widow there was little help to be had from people of my own age, most of whom have little or no knowledge of the realms of grief. We live in a society which regards death as a defeat for medical science rather than a part of life. In a culture which allows little place for death in the pub- lic arena, grief becomes a private affair, viewed as a luxury we cannot afford. We are all amateurs at grief, although sooner or later every one of us will lose someone close to us. I was deter- mined to permit myself the luxury of grieving.

The term 'tacit knowledge' is an interesting one for anyone wish- ing to do more research into mushroom odours. Tacit knowledge is knowledge which a person employs without thinking about it. Language is a good example. People who speak a language fluently could be said to have tacit knowledge of the language. They know how to speak the language, but the majority would not be able to explain the grammatical rules they are using. Tacit knowledge is hard to pass on. One of the best ways of acquiring it, though, is by drawing on the experience of the experts, in the same way that apprentices learn their trade by working alongside skilled craftsmen. Observation, imitation and practice, these are the keys. And practice, as we know, makes perfect. Tacit knowledge is knowledge that has been *physicalised* — become ingrained. Such knowledge can't be picked up from books, which is why written descriptions of how a mushroom smells are only of limited value. Odours have to be smelled and experienced again and again, until the knowledge of them becomes second nature to the novice mushroomer and can be put to practical use. It's all about gaining enough experience to know *how* the Goatcheese Webcap smells and not necessarily of *what*. Do that and you have cracked the aroma code as it is defined by the community. Only then can you understand what everyone else is talking about.

The art of catching mice

When Eiolf died, I also lost access to all the things he knew and could do. Not just his tacit knowledge, but his other skills as well. He had an inquiring mind, he was well and widely read, and he remembered what he read. He was everyone's favourite quiz partner. So whenever I had a question, I could be sure of an interesting answer from him. He had a logical turn of mind and his huge font of knowledge made him the ideal sparring partner.

'What would Eiolf have said or done?' is a question I have frequently asked myself. The answers I arrive at give me ideas and the strength to try them out. This applies not just to the big, serious issues, but also to the little challenges of everyday life — such as catching mice. This was not a subject of which I had any knowledge, tacit or practical. However, I recently crossed the line between knowing, in theory, how to catch mice and actually catching a mouse. To anyone who has a hunting licence and has felled very large animals a wee mouse is obviously peanuts. But not to me. Don't get me wrong, I'm not like the women in comic strips from the 1950s, jumping onto a stool and screaming 'Eeek!' at the sight of a mouse, but in our house there were some jobs which were mine and some which were Eiolf's, and catching mice was definitely not my department. He saw to that, and I never had to worry about it.

There was a real edge to the air. Autumn was on the way, no doubt about it. Nor was there any doubt that the faint scrabbling sounds I had heard in the middle of the night meant a mouse or two had moved into the cottage at the allotment. The little boxroom containing the boiler offered a warm, snug alternative to a cold existence outside in the autumn night. I wasn't much for it, but I knew I would have to do something. There was no putting it off, no way round it. Deep down I knew that I was going to have to dig out Eiolf's favourite 'Giljotti' mousetrap, which instantly breaks the neck of any mouse that ventures to take the bait. I'm ashamed to admit it, but I spent a while turning this killing machine one way and another, trying to figure out how it worked. That's what happens when you haven't played with Lego and Meccano as a child. I used a small twig to test the mechanism, feeling clever and cunning. What should I use as bait? Bacon, would that tempt a mouse? Bacon it was. I set the trap in the boxroom and settled down in the bedroom next door. There was to be a lunar eclipse that night, the last for decades, so everyone was waiting for that. But I was waiting for the mouse.

At 1.30am I heard rodent ructions in the boxroom. I held my breath, ears straining. It's amazing how sharp our hearing can become when we are really listening for a particular sound. I lay in bed, stiff as a board — tense, ears straining, with only a thin wood-panelled wall between the mouse and me. It wasn't pleasant, having to lie there listening to the little creature's death throes being played out behind my pillow. Eventually, after what seemed like an eternity, all was quiet. I breathed a sigh of relief.

The question which immediately presented itself was how was I to get rid of the hapless mouse, but that could wait till the morning. I have no plans to become a great mouse-catcher, but this just goes to show: needs must when the devil — or in this case the rodent — drives.

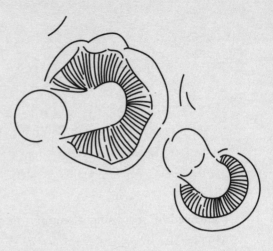

An aroma
seminar

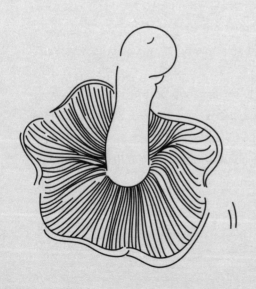

I dreamed of organising a seminar on mushroom odours, at which smell specialists from *outside* the mushroom community could tell us what *they* smell when they nose different fungi. Specimens would be handed round one by one, for these non-mushroomers to sniff at, as we always do. But how to organise something like that? Where to find individuals with well-trained noses and an extensive olfactory vocabulary?

I met M. at a party in Paris. He works in the perfume industry, his main project being to build up a database of scents of relevance to the business. A man he knew popped in to the party to say hello. M. hugged him, identified his fragrance, and complimented him on his choice of cologne — it was perfect for him, he said. I was tremendously impressed by M.'s scent detection skills. He had reminded me that individual chemical reactions to perfumes vary. The same fragrance can smell quite different on different people. So his compliment was not just for the cologne, but for the combination of the cologne and the man.

The global market for products to make us smell nice is enormous, as numerous international celebrities have discovered.

The classic perfume brands now have to compete with the likes of Britney Spears, Beyoncé, Rihanna, Jennifer Lopez, and Celine Dion, all of whom have launched their own perfumes. We give a great deal of thought to the way we smell. Not only do we spend a lot of money on fragrances to spray or dab on our bodies, there is also a big market for products to banish other unwanted bodily odours.

I told M. about the problems I was having with mushroom odours and how I found it hard to identify certain aroma descriptors. He did not think this was a problem, it was simply a matter of practice, practice, and more practice. He tried to illustrate this by giving me a brief introduction to his world. Just as all colours can be split into the primary colours, scents can be broken down into large 'primary fragrance families' such as oriental, citrus, floral, or woody. Within each family there are several variations of the fragrance. The contents of all the perfume bottles in our own homes are likely to be dominated by one fragrance family because as individuals we tend to favour a particular range of notes. Perfume experts use terms from the music world, frequently referring to the top, middle, and base notes in a perfume, and speaking of the combination of these as a 'harmony'. According to M., some perfumes may be composed of only two or three elements, like a musical duo or trio, while other, more complex, fragrances could be likened to an entire orchestra of olfactory elements.

Could mushroom odours also be described as musical harmonies? Might some be compared to simple song ensembles and others to a big band? My head buzzed with questions as I listened to M. One thing that mushrooms, music, and wine have in common is that there is so much information to absorb, and everyone who enjoys these three has their own particular tastes. M. also had an explanation for why serious mushroomers always stick their nose right up against the mushroom, a habit which it had taken me some time to get used to. Before we can smell anything, the smellable molecules have to be carried through the air to our noses. When we open our nostrils to sniff the mushroom these molecules travel up to the top of the nose, where we have a membrane containing receptors which pick them up. All of this happens in the *olfactory epithelium*, a tiny area of around one and a half square inches that can detect and discriminate between an infinite number of odours. It translates them into chemical signals which are transmitted straight to the brain.

'It's all just chemistry, really,' M. said.

When the linguist Asifa Majid compared the language of the Jahai, a hunter-gatherer tribe, with English, she found that the Jahai language had a much wider vocabulary to describe smells. In Jahai, for example, there are very specific words for the smell of old rice, mushrooms, boiled cabbage, and certain birds. No one is quite sure why this should be, but Majid suggests that it could be because to survive in the jungle the sense of smell has to be as highly developed as the sense of sight.

It has been said that if dogs could talk we wouldn't be able to understand them. Some researchers believe that dogs read and interpret all the elements of the surrounding smellscape at once, as do bees — a skill which enables them to locate the flowers they need. Professionals in the perfume business use very particular words to pin down and define subtle variations in scents. For those who don't speak the language of the perfumer these words mean nothing. We don't know that 'aromatic' means 'notes of camphor and herbs such as lavender, rosemary, and sage'. All perfumers employ the same descriptors: adjectives such as amber, animalic, camphorous, creamy, cool, fatty, grassy, leathery, oriental, petally, powdery, soapy. They have their own, more specialist jargon for describing scents. That, I believe, is the crux of the matter.

Insider lingo

In an article in *The New Yorker* John Lanchester describes how it took him a long time to figure out what other wine connoisseurs meant when they spoke of a wine being 'grainy'. Initially this quality eluded him, because he didn't have the words to describe it. Then one day he got it, suddenly he understood what everyone else had been talking about. As he himself put it: 'I took a sip ... and *bam!*' From then on he could discuss with other wine connoisseurs, who spoke the same language, the fact that he found a wine grainy. They could all associate that particular taste experience with this term.

Once you're on the inside of a subculture and privy to a more precise common language, it is easy to forget what it was like to be an outsider. To the uninitiated, all that wine buff talk of roses and kerosene, butter, horsehide, cherries, and tar might seem like nothing but hot air and snobbery. We outsiders can neither see, taste, or smell what the insiders are talking about. From the outside it can easily resemble a scene from *The Emperor's New Clothes*. In the case of both perfume fragrances and wine bouquets we're talking about a technical jargon with its own very specific terminology. What confuses the issue somewhat is that the terms they use are not new. They are everyday words which have been accorded new specialised meanings. Learn to understand the new applications of these words and you will have broken through the culture barrier.

To crack the Norwegian outdoor code you not only have to learn the language, but also and most importantly, this cultural construct has to become second nature to you. The communication of perfume, wine, or mushroom scents may have something in common with the crossing of similar cultural barriers. When such barriers are crossed, through revelations of a sort in which the jigsaw pieces of the new knowledge fall into place, there is no going back. This new knowledge cannot be unlearned.

Having poured the wine, experts close their eyes, stick their noses deep into the glass, and inhale. They shut out everything around them and concentrate solely on the scents filling their nostrils. Which aromas do they smell and recognise? Which of these aromas resemble those already stored in their mental aroma banks? First they sniff the wine while it is lying still in the glass, then they give it a swirl and sniff it again. When the wine is swirled, the aromas — volatile chemical compounds — surge straight up the nose, which is strategically positioned in the middle of the glass. Wine expert Ingvild Tennfjord compares swirling the wine to turning up the volume on a piece of music. The aromas almost 'explode' in the nostrils in what is a highly sensual experience. And, as Tennfjord says, if you can smell the wine better, it will also taste better.

How do oenologists, or wine experts, train their noses? They are constantly working to increase their catalogue of olfactory memories. Scents are memorised and tucked away in their aroma banks. Tennfjord suggests half filling a wine glass with strawberries, say, then sticking your nose into the glass to truly smell and memorise the scent of strawberries. You may think you know how strawberries smell, but this exercise can help you to discover fresh sensory impressions, because the smell in the glass is so concentrated. Then compare the smell of strawberries with that of raspberries, for example. And so on, systematically training your wine nose and expanding your olfactory repertoire.

Dogs can be trained to become special truffle hounds. Could we train our mushroom noses in the same way? What if we took an assortment of different mushrooms, each with a distinctive odour, and put them into a series of wine glasses. Each glass would capture and concentrate the aroma of its own mushroom. Once we were sure of the aroma in one glass, we could move on to the next. Another good exercise would be to check how many mushrooms you can identify by smell alone — by sniffing them blindfolded, for example. Maybe the Society should consider having a 'blind sniffing' competition at the next annual mushroom fair. As a start, I would suggest filling the row of wine glasses to the brim with mushrooms which smell of flour, semen, apricots, radishes, freshly-baked coconut macaroons, almonds, soft soap, shellfish, raw potato, artificial sweetener, barbecue smoke, and curry.

My idea for an aroma seminar was taken up by The Greater Oslo Fungi and Useful Plants Society, but the Society's limited budget didn't stretch to inviting a professional perfumer or oenologist. I was very keen, though, to have the mushroom odours described by a well-trained nose, one that had not been socialised to the standard descriptors used by the mushroom community. What were we to do?

A sensory panel

The solution presented itself in the form of a sensory panel. A sensory panel uses the human senses to assess and describe the attributes of a product, in terms of colour, form, smell, taste, texture, sound, and pain. This last relates to foods such as chilli, which do actually cause pain due to their hotness. Such panels are made up of groups of professional sensory profilers, super-tasters whose senses are inherently more acute than the average person's.

The funny thing was that the members of the panel were also intrigued by this assignment, because they had never worked with mushrooms before. So it was a win-win situation. Obviously, though, we would have to confine ourselves to whichever mushrooms were available on the day when the panel was due to conduct the test.

The panel was presented with samples of mushrooms which, according to mushroom gatherers, should all have very different and distinctive odours. The most thorough and comprehensive sensory analysis technique is called *descriptive profiling*. First, a product's attributes are *identified* in a brainstorming session. In stage two the panel reach agreement on the *intensity* of each of the product's attributes. Our aroma seminar focused only on the first part of this process, the brainstorming session. The panel pinpointed the attributes which they all agreed to be characteristic of each mushroom. They did not, however, have the time or the opportunity to reach any conclusion on the intensity of each attribute.

The panel's results were as follows:

Mushroom	According to the sensory panel	According to Norwegian mushroom guides
Clitopilus prunulus Miller Mushroom	Wood, cardboard, cucumber	Green, mealy
Hydnellum suaveolens (No common English name)	Lavender, aniseed, sweet, chemicals, coconut, perfume	Pleasant scent
Lactarius helvus Fenugreek Milk Cap	Curry, rubber, brown sugar, burnt odour, spices	Curry, stock cube, lovage, fennel, coumarin
Amanita porphyria Grey Veiled Amanita	Earthy, musty, nuts, potato, turnip	Raw potato
Macrocystidia cucumis Cucumber Cap	Fish, salt water, salmon, cucumber	Cucumber, fish
Inocybe geophylla White Fibrecap	Ammonia, metal, moss, earth, grass	Spermatic
Lactarius gylciosmus Coconut Milk Cap	Rubber, diesel oil, pencil erasers, coconut, spicy, moss, musty, mould	Freshly baked coconut macaroons
Cortinarius paleaceus Pelargonium Webcap	Earth, bark, metal, moss	Geraniums
Lepiota cristata Stinking Dapperling	Chemicals, earth, nauseating	Unpleasant chemical smell

Russula xerampelina Crab Brittlegill	Ammonia, rotten fish	Fish (herring)
Russula violeipes Velvet Brittlegill	Plastic, fish, moss	Shellfish
Agaricus arvensis Horse Mushroom	Liquorice, forest	Almonds
Agaricus sylvicola Wood Mushroom	Liquorice, burnt odour, aniseed, moss, ammonia, earthy	Almonds
Cantharellus cibarius Chanterelle	Carrot, turpentine, sweet, forest, moss	Dried apricots
Hebeloma crustuliniforme Poison Pie	Earthy, musty, forest floor	Radish-like
Hebeloma sacchariolens Sweet Poison Pie	Synthetic sweets, medicine, linoleum, new car	Sweet, fruity, strong
Entoloma rhodopolium Wood Pinkgill	Soft soap, mould, pine	Soapy

From the sensory panel's first session with the mushrooms, we can see that it agrees with the descriptions given in Norwegian field guides in just 50 per cent of cases.

This made me wonder about the descriptions given in mushroom guides from other countries. A quick and fairly random review of North American field guides revealed, among other things, that the Miller Mushroom, as well as having a 'mealy odour' is reported as smelling 'somewhat like cucumber', a description I have never come across in Norwegian guides. I also found the Grey Veiled Amanita described as smelling of radish and turnip. In these cases the sensory panel seemed to have detected aromas that the Americans had also sniffed out.

This little exercise shows that the accepted Norwegian truths on mushroom odours should not necessarily be taken as gospel. Even though the ten panellists spent four hours on this first phase — the equivalent of a full working week — there is clearly more work to be done. It would have been great if we could have continued our collaboration with the sensory panel. But perhaps even these preliminary findings will help us to see that we still have a way to go in terms of describing the olfactory attributes of the mushrooms we know. Perhaps they will encourage us to refine our mushroom noses, or simply encourage the general interest in mushrooms and fungi.

Wine, cheese, beer, coffee, and olive oil all have their own internationally standardised aroma wheels, which describe the mouthfeel, the smell, and the taste of products. A standardised aroma wheel makes it easier to convey one's findings. For example, when wine experts talk of a caramel aroma they can then go on to specify exactly which sort of caramel they mean — be it molasses, chocolate, butter, butterscotch, or honey. Imagine if mushrooms had their very own aroma wheel!

In Norway, all the fungi native to the country are now being barcoded as part of the global Barcode of Life project. It is one thing to digitalise the DNA of all the world's fungi, quite another to describe the analogue experience of a mushroom's aroma. Why do we lack the lexicon and the language to describe mushroom odours more precisely? When I discussed this with a mycologist from the Natural History Museum at the University of Oslo he presented one theory: the famous Swedish mycologist Elias Fries is regarded as the father of mushroom classification. Fries' works *Systema Mycologicum* (1821–1832), *Elenchus Fungorem* (1828), *Monographia Hymenomycetum Sueciae* (1857, 1863) and *Hymenomycetes Europaei* (1874) have assured him of his place as a major — if not *the* major — contributor to modern mycological taxonomy. But Fries was a cigar smoker and smoking, as we know, affects our sense of smell.

How good was Fries' sense of smell, I wonder?

Old habits and new

Of the bereaved individuals I know, some stopped smoking the moment their loved one died, while others took up the habit again. Fortunately I have never fallen prey either to tobacco's kick or its curse. As a child I was offered a puff of a cigarette by my dad, a non-smoker — a cunning way, as it turned out, of rendering me immune to the insidious charms of smoking.

The Fransiskushhelpen invited our bereavement group to an evening talk by one widow on how she had gradually built up a new life for herself. There were two comfortable armchairs on the platform, one for the speaker and one for a representative of the organisation. The person from the Fransiskushjelpen asked questions, the widow replied. It was an interesting evening, but what surprised me was that it was 10 years since this woman had lost her husband. Ten whole years. What an awful long time to be in mourning, I thought.

Some of us grieve for our loved ones longer than others, but for everyone it takes time for the pieces to fall into place and form a new picture. Language is one of these pieces. The first thing I had to learn was to use the right tense: when speaking of Eiolf I now had to use the past tense, not the present. To begin with, this seemed all wrong because he was still there, all around me. It also took time to figure out when it was correct to use 'we' and when the personal pronoun was more appropriate. I think the most difficult thing to say was the name of my company, Long & Olsen, and having to be prepared, when I met new customers, to explain who the 'Olsen' referred to. For a while I even considered changing the company's name simply to avoid being put in what was — for me — a difficult situation. My professionalism demanded that I act as though I was done mourning, when in fact I was still bobbing about in a cheap, dodgy rubber dinghy on the high seas of grief.

When does one actually cease to mourn? And how many long, relentless hours does it take? Grief is a hard taskmaster.

Gathering one's senses

To know your mushrooms you have to train all of your senses, not least your sense of smell, in order to take in all the information necessary to determine a mushroom's species. This was something I found difficult because, in addition to being a novice, my sensory faculties had been numbed by grief. Could it be that my absorption in mushroom lore and learning also speeded up my return to life by reactivating my senses? To start sensing the world again was like waking from a hundred-year sleep. To sense was to be present, both physically and mentally. When forced to use my senses in different ways, I gradually ceased to observe my widowhood from the outside and slowly got to grips with my own life. And perhaps this just shows how closely linked my two journeys — the involuntary excursion into the labyrinth of grief and the utterly voluntary foray into the mushroom field — have been.

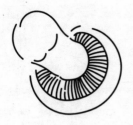

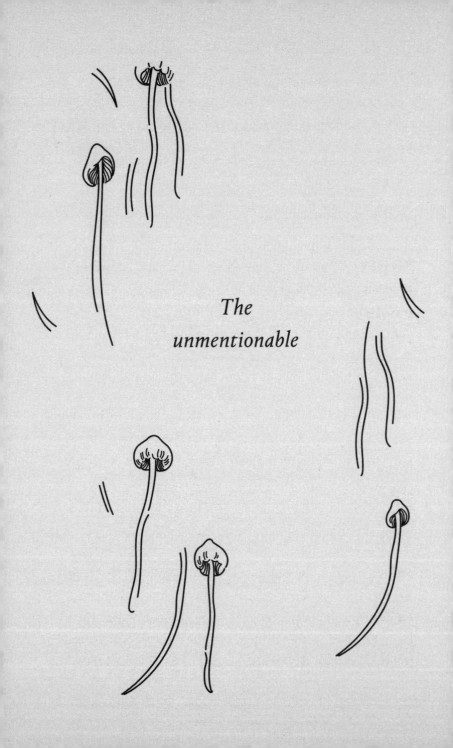

The
unmentionable

Key the word 'mushroom' into Google and you will immediately be bombarded with pages, not on edible mushrooms, but on the psychedelic sort. Fungi with hallucinogenic properties are what the mushroom hunters of cyberspace are most interested in. It is widely believed that there is a link between Viking berserkers and the ingestion of certain mushrooms. Another popular myth is that Sami shamans drank the urine of reindeer who had eaten Fly Agaric. Although it is true that reindeer urine has been used as medicine by Sami healers, I'm afraid there is little foundation for these beguiling ideas of Vikings or Samis ingesting hallucinogenic mushrooms. Many people, myself included, are actually very disappointed that there is no research to back up these weird rumours.

When we were students, Eiolf had a friend who was hellbent on smoking whatever came his way, hoping to get stoned. His dream was to find Liberty Caps, otherwise known as magic mushrooms. He never stopped talking about 'shrooms', although I don't think he ever got any further than growing his own 'special' tobacco plants. I, for one, had never laid eyes on a Liberty Cap back then.

The mushroom that must not be named

For centuries, people have been fascinated by the unique properties of psilocybin mushrooms. When the father of ethno-mycology, Robert Gordon Wasson visited Mexico in the 1950s he was told that there were around 50 different *Psilocybe* species in the country. These were used mainly by the local people in sacred rites. Wasson's curiosity was aroused by reports from his sources that these divine Mexican mushrooms, 'Carry you there where God is'*('Le llevan ahí donde Dios está').*

When, after some years as a novice, I was preparing for the mushroom inspector's exam, I not only read the set texts, but every other book on mushrooms and fungi I could get hold of. I had worked my way through a huge pile of books before I sud-denly came across a picture of a Liberty Cap in a field guide. For some reason I had never associated the Liberty Cap — which I had first heard of years before — with my new interest in mush-rooms. So I was a little taken aback.

What surprised me was how small and unremarkable the fungus in the picture seemed. It looked so ordinary, this legend-ary mushroom, and not very exciting — it was hard to imagine it being in any way 'magic'. It struck me that none of the books on mushrooms I had read so far had contained any pictures of Liberty Caps. Which was odd. I leafed through all the books again and this time I checked the index of each one, looking specifically for entries on the Liberty Cap. A few had dedicated a brief line or two to *Psilocybe semilanceata*, which I had missed first time round, but there were no illustrations of Liberty Caps to be found. How come?

When one considers the enormous online interest in psychoactive mushrooms, the silence evinced by field guides on our local psilocybin species is almost deafening. It could, of course, just be coincidence that the books I looked at had accorded no space to the Liberty Cap. I'm not normally a fan of conspiracy theories, but what if that's what this *was*? Might there be some sort of tacit agreement within mushroom circles and among field guide writers to keep information on psilocybins under wraps? Could there possibly be a desire to deliberately prevent people from learning how to correctly identify the Liberty Cap. This outrageous thought reeked of conspiracy and collusion.

I put my theory to one of the senior members of my local society, who assured me most emphatically that there was absolutely no agreement of any sort, formal or informal, to withhold information. But when I asked him if there was anyone in the association whom I could interview, in order to learn more about psilocybin mushrooms, he looked so appalled that I realised I had hit a nerve. Did I know, he retorted, that if you ate psilocybin mushrooms you ran the risk of falling into a coma that you might never come out of.

This response, which seemed a little out of proportion, put me on my guard. There is little doubt that the Liberty Cap is taboo as far as society at large is concerned, but apparently displaying any hint of interest in this species was beyond the pale of the mushrooming community as well. Maybe I was naïve, but I had expected more mycological information and less emotion from one of the association's elder statesmen. But he did not put me off with the supposed information he gave me, which clearly had only one aim: to nip my interest in the bud. To be honest, this only made me even more curious.

I decided to find out more from other, hopefully more neutral, sources. Was there anyone who didn't have a hidden agenda when it came to the Liberty Cap? Or did this controversial fungus split the mushroom world into two camps — the friends of *Psilocybe semilanceata* and its foes — each with their own version of the truth?

I had quite a job finding someone willing to talk to me about taking Liberty Caps, but after several attempts I finally managed to set up an initial meeting with someone in the know.

I arrived at St Olavs plass, in the centre of Oslo, at the appointed time, feeling a little nervous. The person I was there to meet, N., was not known to me personally. A mutual acquaintance had put me in touch with him. I sat down next to the café's large window and watched the people walking past outside. Was that him? That man plodding by with a cigarette butt dangling from his lower lip and a newspaper tucked under his arm? Or that middle-aged gentleman, greying slightly at the temples, who looked rather nice? Or what about the guy in the overcoat, strolling along, clearly in no hurry, in the middle of the day? He obviously had no job to go to. I could almost picture him creeping around the city's graveyards, hunting for Liberty Caps. I had no idea how N. looked or how old he was. I had checked his mobile number before leaving home and a totally different name had come up. Could N. be an assumed name? Several other potential candidates came along, but none of them appeared to be looking for someone in particular. Five minutes after the agreed time I decided to call him. The moment I pressed the 'call' button on my phone the mobile of the young man sitting next to me started to wail: his ringtone was the sound of a police siren. N. had been there all the time, so near and yet so far away.

We said a hesitant hello. I was surprised that he was so young. Slim, his skin smooth and youthful. His hair was tousled, but maybe that's the fashion these days, I thought. Style-wise, his hair matched the rest of him: he wore a battered leather jacket, ripped and frayed and studded with buttons, and tight black jeans that sat low on his skinny hips. N. was a regular magic mushroom user. He spoke softly, seemed rather shy. Does taking magic mushrooms turn a person into an introvert?

I thanked him for agreeing to speak to me and said I would like to hear more about his experiences with psilocybin mushrooms. As an anthropologist I'm used to having to coax people to talk, but N. needed no encouragement. Once he started there was no stopping him. To him 'mushrooms' was short for 'magic mushrooms'. According to N., two to three mushrooms is the right dosage. He lowered his voice even further and informed me that he had actually taken a couple before coming to meet me. I was interested to know how often he took such a dose. Once every month or so, he said. This surprised me, I had thought it would be more often, but that may say more about my own ignorance of mushroom tripping than anything else. We had met at two o'clock in the afternoon, so N. was possibly still high when talking to me, but I would have never guessed; he seem perfectly clear-headed.

Psilocybe semilanceata,
Liberty Caps or magic mushrooms

Professor Høiland puts psilocybins into perspective

I was delighted to discover that Professor Klaus Høiland, to whom I had spoken previously about poisonous mushrooms, had also written scientific articles specifically on the Liberty Cap. It was time for another meeting over coffee at the University of Oslo's Department of Biosciences.

Professor Høiland began by emphasising that Liberty Caps are *not* addictive. Nor are they among our most toxic mushrooms. I mentioned that I had been told recently about the danger of falling into a permanent coma, but this only made him laugh.

'Somebody really said that?' he asked, grinning.

Høiland went on to tell me that what makes the Liberty Cap so controversial is its powerful hallucinogenic effect. The substances psilocin and psilocybin, toxins similar to LSD both in structure and effect, are what render these mushrooms psychoactive. They have a direct impact on the central nervous system and can also affect the user's psychomotor responses. Various sensory impressions may become confused or persist long after the stimulus is gone. Perceptions of light, sound, and smell can, therefore, be different from how they would normally be. The function of the brain is altered and this leads to temporary changes in sentience, mood, awareness, or behaviour, but there is still much to be learned about the way in which these substances affect the brain and the state of mind. The influence does not wear off until the toxin is out of the system. There is little doubt, however, that such effects are pretty potent.

Worldwide, there are about 200 species of mushroom which contain the tryptamines psilocin and psilocybin, most of them belonging to the genus *Psilocybe*. These are, for the most part, small and puny. They are saprophytes, which is to say that they grow on dead organic matter such as manure, rotting wood and plants, humus, and moss. Damp fields and riding school paddocks are also good psilocybin hunting grounds.

'There are magic mushrooms in Grønland Park in Oslo, next to the prison,' is a statement I heard many a time when I was trying to drum up some reliable sources. Although this may have been more a reflection of the prison inmates' dreams than actual fact. I have never checked whether it is true.

Impartial information or incitement to mass psychedelia?

In Norway, the Liberty Cap is the psilocybin of choice for the majority of mushroom trippers. It is covered by the Norwegian law governing narcotics, according to which anyone who 'illegally manufactures, imports, exports, acquires, stores, trafficks, or dispenses substances regarded by law as narcotics will be charged under the Controlled Drugs and Substances Act and be liable to a fine and/or imprisonment for up to two years'.

The aim of mycological societies is to promote the knowledge of mushrooms and fungi, but on the subject of Liberty Caps opinions are divided. On the one hand, Professor Høiland and other mycologists have, over the years, written various articles on psilocybins and other related species for the Norwegian Mycological Association's magazine. I also attended an annual national mushroom festival at which Professor Høiland gave a talk on the hallucinogenic effects of the Liberty Cap. On the other, I have seen the way veterans of my local society pull down the shutters as soon as I start to ask too many questions.

One can see how the fear of legal repercussions might move these pillars of the mushroom community to keep mum on the subject of Liberty Caps — and hope that any flicker of curiosity will be stifled by the lack of reliable information. But this tactic of dissociating oneself from 'shrooms' and expressing one's abhorrence of them also has to be viewed in the wider cultural context. It seems to tie in with the central philosophy behind the Norwegian policy on drink and drugs in general, this being to protect people from themselves. The authorities either declare intoxicating substances illegal or endeavour to restrict potential damage from them by setting age limits for purchase and consumption and having state-controlled sales outlets.

As a newcomer to the country, the Norwegian government's measures to combat heavy drinking came as a shock to me. The idea that anyone, whatever their age, should be able to purchase alcohol at any time of the day is unthinkable in Norway. Such a thing could have only one outcome: namely, that this peace-loving people would run amok. Having grown up in a country with a totally different attitude to alcohol, I knew that this assumption was based more on culturally conditioned reasoning and learned reflexes than anything else.

As far as Liberty Caps are concerned, some people seem to believe that any information on them which does not act as a deterrent is as good as an incitement to indulge in criminal activities and mass psychedelia. Consequently, information on psilocybin mushrooms is withheld, a strategy which immediately conjures up images of book burning and the like. It also calls to mind the opposition of certain conservative and religious organisations to education on sex and contraception, their rationale being that such information will only encourage more young people to have sex. These organisations hope that the lack of clear, well-balanced information, combined with the fear of getting pregnant, will prevent inappropriate youthful shenanigans.

The idea that information on psilocybin mushrooms should not be freely available is also common on social media sites dedicated to mushrooms. When a picture of a small mushroom recently appeared with a request for help with identification, attempts were made to play it down, to stifle any potentially unhealthy interest.

Here is a little extract from the thread in question:

'You don't need to learn about that one. Too small to eat.'

'But we're free to learn about any mushroom we like, aren't we?'

'Yeah, but I've a suspicion this is one of the ones that's been banned.'

'Are you thinking of magic mushrooms?'

'Don't answer questions like that here.'

Finally a comment was posted asserting that the pictured fungus was probably a common lawn mushroom, *Panaeolina foenisecii*, a species which has nothing to recommend it in terms of psychoactive properties. This put an end to a fairly typical discussion thread. It's obvious that a lot of people feel there is something immoral about the Liberty Cap, a mushroom so dangerous its name must not be mentioned. Preventing people from wanting to experiment with magic mushrooms is seen as such a noble goal that no one ever questions what is, in effect, social control and the restriction of freedom of speech.

It's really not so surprising that people with an interest in mushrooms want to know about psilocybin mushrooms. It is, after all, the one wild mushroom most of them have heard of — that and the chanterelle. As I see it, the mushroom community is eminently well-placed to provide information on and answer questions about psilocybin mushrooms in a sensible and impartial manner.

How dangerous are Liberty Caps? According to information from the Norwegian health authorities, there is no proof that the ingestion of Liberty Caps has any harmful physical effect, but users can experience a number of adverse psychological effects from the hallucinogen in the mushroom. The hallucinations induced by eating magic mushrooms can be extremely frightening, inasmuch as the individual can experience alarming 'visuals' and an altered sense of reality. This can bring on panic attacks and activate latent mental disorders. For some time afterwards, the user may have flashbacks of things experienced during a trip, something which can give rise to severe feelings of anxiety. These flashbacks are caused by the fact that psilocin is fat-soluble and can therefore be stored in the fatty tissue of the brain, from where it can trigger fresh and unplanned psychedelic trips long after ingestion of the mushrooms, thus putting the user in potentially dangerous situations. Other possible negative effects which have been cited include deep feelings of dread and angst, headaches, confusion, nausea and bowel discomfort, dizziness, and cognitive fragmentation. Conditions such as epilepsy can be exacerbated by a Liberty Cap trip; a bad trip can induce psychosis; and it is not wise to mix alcohol and 'shrooms'. So, all in all, taking magic mushrooms can be a risky business.

Professor Høiland also believes, however, that it is important to put psilocybins into context. As he explains, the substance which tops the list of dangerous drugs worldwide is alcohol, followed by heroin. Psilocybin mushrooms come at the bottom of the list, along with LSD. *Curiouser and curiouser*, I thought to myself, like Alice. I remembered how shocked I had been when I first came to Norway from Malaysia as a young student by the sight of blind drunk Norwegians staggering around the streets on a normal Friday night in town. It took me a long time to learn the Norwegian words for different levels of drunkenness; in Malaysia you're either drunk or sober. It's both interesting and strange that alcohol should be a socially acceptable intoxicant, while the Liberty Cap is classified as a Class A drug. Why this should be so is a question for another time.

Mushroom tripping

What happens during a mushroom trip and how are the mushrooms taken? According to the Norwegian Institute of Public Health, the active ingredient psilocybin can be extracted from magic mushrooms, or they can be eaten fresh, dried, or mixed with food or drink. Information from the health authorities says that users may experience a sense of clarity and heightened sensory awareness. Things may also seem to change shape or colour and the world round about become a weird and wonderful place. Perception of time is impaired and the user may have the impression that the barriers between them and their surroundings melt away, creating a state in which they feel 'at one with everything'. This sensation of being at one with all living things, animals and plants, is a phenomenon often described in literature on the subject.

Psilocybins provoke such negative reactions within my local society that I almost felt I was breaking the rules by even thinking of asking what a mushroom trip was like. But that's what happens when the quashing of politically incorrect ideas is the norm. I took the chance and called N. again.

'What's so good about magic mushrooms?' I asked N. He described a mushroom high as 'cosy'; 'a bit like being tickled by a feather', as he put it. 'A wonderful feeling that lasts all day.' Mushrooms are more 'motherly' than other drugs, according to N., who had clearly had plenty of experience. I asked him to elaborate. He started by saying that it was pointless to try and describe the experience in words because it's 'nothing like the world as we know it', but that the predominant sensation was one of interconnectedness.

Another source, G., told me about a time when he had taken magic mushrooms and was sitting on a hill, gazing out across Oslo. He felt as though the city was a part of him and he was a part of it. The tall old trees he was looking at could have been there for a hundred years or more. His grandfather, or even his great-grandfather, might have known those same trees. And who knew, maybe his own children, grandchildren, or great-grandchildren would see them too. It was all so beautiful, he said, almost spiritual. G. told me how he became like a child again when he took 'caps' as he called them. He asked me if I remembered what it was like, as a child, to see a conjurer produce a rabbit from beneath a top hat. Amazing! That, G. said, was what a mushroom trip was like. But, he hastened to add, one could also experience other, less pleasant, effects. 'What you have to remember, though, is that any adverse reactions you have during the trip will disappear once it's over,' he said.

'Taking magic mushrooms won't make you go mad, but what you unearth when you're high might,' G. said with a smile. 'For example, if you ask yourself what sort of a mother you are, you might get an answer you don't like.'

N. told me that getting high on mushrooms gave him a deeper understanding of the world around him, and that he saw it 'without any filter'.

'It doesn't provide you with any answers, but it helps you to see the world more clearly.' He went on to say that he liked taking magic mushrooms because the transition from a normal state to being high was gradual and he could actually 'see' it happen. According to N., magic mushrooms open up 'a creative field inside you'. It is a holistic and highly physical experience. Yoga, meditation, and dance can also act as paths to this creative field,

N. said., but that could take a little longer. He must be talking about different forms of yoga, meditation or dance than any I've ever tried, I thought to myself. N. then described a psilocybin high as being like 'riding a wave'. As he had grown more experienced he had become more adept at 'finding the wave again', he said. Time became 'elastic', he added. I asked him what he meant by that. He told me that he had more time to reflect on things, because his head 'expanded' and 'stories become bigger'. I found this concept hard to grasp. He tried to explain it by using psychedelic music as an example: listen to it when you're not high on mushrooms and the tempo will seem very upbeat. But if you've taken mushrooms, the music won't seem nearly so fast, because you're viewing it from an 'inner perspective'. Time stretches out and you are able to discern more dimensions of a story than you would otherwise see. N. said that when he took magic mushrooms he found it easier to make decisions because they opened his eyes to subtler aspects of the choice to be made, nuances which he might not have been aware of before.

I had read an interview with another user who said that the experience had made him a better person. It would appear that a psilocybin trip is not regarded purely as a passing fancy or casual recreation, but as a door onto profound experiences which some feel help them to grow as individuals. N. confirmed this, saying that psilocybins made him more sympathetic to other people. They helped him to hear what other people were saying. He believed that they made him more alive to nuances of emotion in others.

N. told me that it was fun to take psilocybins with a group of people: there was little need to talk because they could communicate via telepathy. G. also told me how he became very close to the people he took 'caps' with. According to him, one person should always act as the trip 'mother', who would not get high, but stay clear-headed and look after the rest of the group.

N. had recently heard about truffle hounds and he asked me whether I thought he could train his dog to be a 'shroom hound'. I had no advice to offer on that score, but it seemed as though N. and his friends were managing to rustle up enough 'shrooms' without any help from our four-legged friends.

'Psychedelic' was the word N. used to describe the magic mushroom scene, a word I associated with the 1960s and the hippie movement. I looked it up and found that psychedelics are a sub-category of hallucinogenics. While other sub-categories, such as opiates, cause hallucinations based on things the mind knows from before, psychedelics can induce altered states of consciousness, hence the term 'mind-bending'. The word 'psychedelic' comes from the Greek words *psukhē*, meaning 'mind' or 'soul', and *dēlos*, meaning 'manifest' or 'clear'. Psychedelic experiences can, therefore, be described as 'manifestations of the soul'. The members of the psychedelic scene to which N. belonged shared an interest in art and (loud) music; psychedelic art and psychedelic rock music try to convey the experience of altered consciousness, often through vivid, kaleidoscopic images, surreal visual and sound effects, and animation (as in cartoons). And suddenly I realised, of course, this was what those weird, swirling, colourful patterns on hippie-style T-shirts were all about. And I thought they were just innocent designs.

After lunch we stepped outside so that N. could have a cigarette. I noticed that he smoked organic tobacco and I asked him about this. He told me that he and his friends were into 'optimal health'. N. is also a vegan. Evidently his definition of optimal health also included the ingestion of wild mushrooms. What could be more natural than that?

'How do you take the mushrooms?' I asked. N. told me that he made camomile tea, added the mushrooms to this, and drank it with honey. This is a favourite method among users like N. who don't want to feel too much 'like a bloody junkie'. And tea with honey does sound quite wholesome and healthy.

I asked N. if he had ever had a bad trip on psilocybins. He said that he hadn't, but was at pains to point out that you have to keep your dosage to under 10 mushrooms. He added that, while it can be 'fun' to take as many as 60 to 100 mushrooms, or even more than 100, it can also be 'challenging'. His usual dosage was one or two mushrooms. If he took more than this — three to five 'shrooms', say — he found that his hearing became sharper and he got a greater 'energy kick'. Again, however, he stressed the importance of keeping the dosage under 10 mushrooms — more than that, he said, and you will start to 'vibrate', although I wasn't quite sure what he meant by this.

On one of the many 'shroom' sites on the Internet, a heavier and more experienced user of psilocybins has described the different psilocybin 'trip levels' as follows:

Level 1: Mild stoning effect with some visual enhancement (brighter colours, greater contrasts). Some short-term memory anomalies.

Level 2: Bright colours, visuals (things start to move and breathe etc.), possible appearance of two-dimensional patterns upon shutting eyes. Changes in short-term memory, leading to continual distractive thought patterns. Vast increase in creativity becomes apparent as the natural brain filter is bypassed (thinking outside the box).

Level 3: Very obvious visuals, everything looking curved and/or warped patterns/kaleidoscopes seen on walls and other surfaces. Some mild hallucinations, such as rivers flowing in the grain of wood or 'mother-of-pearl' surfaces. Closed-eye hallucinations become three-dimensional. Synaesthesia (confusion of the senses) occurs, i.e. tasting colours, smelling sounds etc. Time distortions and moments of eternity.

Level 4: Strong hallucinations, i.e. objects morphing into other objects. Destruction or multiple splitting of the ego (things start talking to you or you find that you are feeling contradictory things simultaneously). Some loss of reality. Time becomes

meaningless. Possible out-of-body experiences
(seeing yourself from outside) and extrasensory
perception phenomena. Senses not only confused,
but blending together.

Level 5: Total loss of visual connection with reality.
The senses cease to function in the normal way.
Total loss of ego, merging with space, other objects,
the universe. The loss of reality becomes so severe
that it defies explanation. The earlier levels are
relatively easy to explain in terms of measurable
changes in perception and thought patterns. This
level is different in that the actual universe within
which things are normally perceived ceases to exist!
Satori enlightenment (and other such labels) or the
opposite.

From the way N. describes it, it sounds as if his dosage of
fewer than 10 mushrooms would take him to Level 2 or possibly
Level 3 on the above scale from the self-styled magic mushroom
'Trip Advisor'.

One of the main challenges for active users is the dosage,
since the concentration of psychoactive elements can vary quite
widely from mushroom to mushroom, from region to region. So
a shroom is not necessarily just a shroom. While some people use
the number of mushrooms as a measure, others go by weight,
measuring in grams or ounces. But that still doesn't get round

the problem of varying strength. A mushroom's weight is not necessarily a guide to its potency. Opinions differ on how large a beginner's dose should be. In this respect N. would appear to be pretty careful and conservative. He is also well aware of the problem of varying strengths and has one or two particular spots that he returns to every season to gather his shrooms, although I don't see how that helps, since two mushrooms growing side by side could be quite different in potency. Another source, who grows the Cuban Psilocybe, *Psilocybe cubensis*, in his living room, was happy to share his solution to the problem: all of the psilocybins from one harvest should be dried and then, instead of being eaten whole, they should be ground down into 'shroom flour'. This way, the strength of the various mushrooms is evenly distributed.

Another challenge is presented by more dangerous toxic lookalikes which can be found growing right alongside psilocybins including Liberty Caps. A good example are small fibrecap mushrooms. These contain muscarine, which can cause disturbances in the central nervous system. What these mushrooms have in common with psilocybins is that they are small and have pointed caps. N. knows all about these treacherous *doppelgangers* and says himself that fortunately he has never taken a 'wrong mushroom'. But one can imagine that others on the same mission might not have been so lucky.

I came across an article written by Professor Klaus Høiland in which he says that, until 1977, the Liberty Cap was just one of many anonymous little fungi mentioned in field guides. Due to its modest size, its edibility was never checked. But then, in

1977, the Liberty Cap's hallucinogenic properties became known to the Norwegian public. The press had a field day with this news, with tabloid headlines such as 'Dope Mushroom Found in Norway' and 'Psychedelic Pizza'.

So it wasn't just my imagination. There actually was something a bit odd about the absence of any mention of the Liberty Cap from more recent Norwegian field guides. My suspicions regarding a tacit agreement by the writers of mushroom guides can be traced back to Professor Høiland's reference to those tabloid headlines. Mushroomers are advised not to refer to older field guides because information on fungi is regularly rendered obsolete by new research findings. But as far as the Liberty Cap is concerned, anyone interested in learning how to identify it will find what they seek in second-hand bookshops.

Professor Høiland also acts as an advisor on mushrooms and fungi to Norway's National Criminal Investigation Service (KRIPOS). This means that he can monitor changes in the sorts of mushrooms being seized by the police. In recent years, police impoundment records have shown that foreign mushrooms are now finding their way into Norway. This is probably due to the purchase of Cuban Psilocybe and Hawaiian Blue Meanie, *Panaeolus cyanescens*, spores to grow at home. In 2011, the last year when mushrooms were included in police impoundment records, 2.2 kilograms of psilocybin mushrooms were seized by the police (as opposed to 2,976 kilograms of cannabis). In 2014, two people were arrested and charged with production and possession of 100 to 150 grams of narcotic mushrooms (species unspecified). In any case, these figures show that psilocybins are probably not the most commonly used drug in Norway. Impoundment records also show that the mushrooming establishment's strategy of keeping people in the dark about psilocybin mushrooms has only had a limited effect. Anyone who really wants to get high on mushrooms will always find a way.

To prevent accidents or anyone coming to harm due to mistakenly taking dangerous lookalikes, what is needed above all is clear and reliable information, not silence and denial. In the meantime, those wishing to get high and have a psychedelic experience through the intentional ingestion of the psilocybin toxin are doomed to carry on creeping around the hedges in graveyards or along roadsides and grassy fields and figuring out the dosage through trial and error. If they have any questions their only recourse will be to online sources such as the Norwegian Freak Forum or the Erowid website.

In the 1960s, when the hippie counterculture was at its height on university campuses in many Western countries, Terence McKenna and his brother Dennis became known for their book *Psilocybin: Magic Mushroom Grower's Guide*. According to the McKenna brothers, the psilocybin species *Psilocybe cubensis* was particularly easy to grow. All of this was brought to an abrupt halt in 1968, when the substances psilocin and psilocybin were put into the same category as heroin and cocaine and declared illegal in the United States. Research into psychoactive substances being conducted at Harvard and other universities was cut short around the same time.

What is interesting is that research into psilocin and psilocybin from the 1990s is now back on the academic agenda, among other places at the Norwegian University of Science and Technology's Institute for Neuromedicine and Movement Science. In 2008, the British medical journal *The Lancet*, published an article entitled 'Research on psychedelics moves into the mainstream'. Present day studies on psilocybin mushrooms have picked up where research conducted before they were banned left off, focusing on more practical medicinal uses: as an aid to stopping smoking, for example, and to combat depression, PTSD, alcoholism, migraines, and the fear of dying in terminally ill cancer patients.

Despite the Society's strong links with academia, I still have the sneaking suspicion that this new research is unlikely to meet with the approval of its influential senior members.

From starter
to dessert

The traces of a life are all around me. It was strange to look at the bookcase after I had removed Eiolf's books from it. It had never occurred to me that a bookcase could be a symbol of a marriage, but suddenly I saw that our bookcase was just that, with the books we had each collected over a long life of reading mixed up together on the shelves. They weren't arranged under 'my books' and 'his books'. They weren't really arranged in any order. Some books had only been read by one of us, others we had both read. And then there were the ones, I remember, that we would both be reading at the same time and there would be a fight over whose turn it was to have the book. Among these were some of Isaac Bashevis Singer's works. Singer wrote about life in a typical Jewish *shtetl*, a predominantly Yiddish-speaking village in Eastern Europe, before the First World War. His works focus mainly on life and the human experience, on everyday dilemmas and the stories of ordinary people. Singer is a brilliant storyteller and his books bear reading more than once. I kept some of Eiolf's books, the rest I knew I would never read. He read a great deal, both fiction and non-fiction. Not to mention books on war, which only a pacifist like him could find interesting. But then, there were few subjects that didn't interest him. He used to say that his epitaph should read 'Here lie masses of study credits'. That was a typical remark from him. I always forget the punchlines of jokes, so he could tell the same one again and again. Old jokes became new again. It's things like this that make life fun, even after many years together. On his bedside table he left a great pile of books that he meant to read: a fair indication that he hadn't been planning on dying so soon. But the books on the bedside table remain unread. I leafed through them, one by one, and tried my best to be honest with myself: would I ever read them? I gave most of them away.

Reading a book is like taking a walk through an unknown country. It hurts to think of all the books and all the walks that Eiolf never read, never took, and never got to tell me about.

The mathematics of loss

What is it that's gone? It's difficult to calculate, even a Nobel laureate in mathematics would find it hard to come up with an answer to that question. When two individuals decide to live together they create something that is more than the sum of its parts. When one of them passes away, what made the couple unique is lost, but something happens to the one who is left behind as well. When lives and identities have been so closely intertwined, the bereaved partner can be left feeling like a shadow of themselves. We are the ones who pay the price for having found our soul mate. We are the ones who, in effect, have the blessing of that sense of belonging branded into us.

According to some sort of inexplicable balance sheet, what is lost is more valuable than what remains. Gone, too, is the joint stewardship of shared memories. Sole responsibility for these was dumped in my lap when Eiolf died and it weighs heavy. If I forget, our years together will also disappear. Gone are our dreams for the future; into a drawer with them. And that common sphere in which we could relax completely, be each other's best friend, be ourselves — that too will disappear.

Eiolf grew up in a home where the dinner schedule for the week was pretty predictable. Every Monday they had dish A, Tuesday it was dish B; the passage of time and the days of the week marked by each evening meal. It was the same story in many of the homes around him when he was growing up. Mealtimes were no place for extravagance or experimentation, nor were they a goal in themselves. Anything but. Dinner was about eating up and clearing away. And once the table had been wiped and the washing up done, Mum and Dad could finally put their feet up in front of the telly.

My in-laws came from farming stock, but they had embraced modern life and, not least, the new frozen foods and ready-made meals. Maybe that, together with a hunger for new tastes, was why Eiolf took to Malaysian food the way he did. In Malaysia, while people are eating one meal they are planning the next, and they will happily make a long detour just to have dinner. Malaysians have a mental map of places connected with dishes they are known for. Eiolf had been talking for a while about writing a cookbook and calling it *My Mother-in-Law's Kitchen*. I've a suspicion it would have remained unopened in the family home in Stavanger, where no one ate chicken or mushrooms. As a child, the first time Eiolf ate pineapple it was in a slice of layer cake at someone else's house and he threw up. But together with me he went on a gastronomic journey to a land where the pineapple actually grows. Eiolf loved to shock his family with tales of licking braised chicken feet, sucking the insides out of steamed fish eyes, and sampling other exotic delights in distant climes. East met West in our kitchen long before fusion cuisine became trendy. That was fine by Eiolf. He could always have Norwegian food at his mum and dad's.

The fridge is another reminder of our life together. As in all households, we accommodated each other's tastes in food. Over the years we had gradually banished from the kitchen certain ingredients which one or other of us could not stand. Conversely, we tended to eat a lot more of those things that we both liked. Eiolf wasn't as keen on aubergines as I am. Or chickpeas. He wasn't mad about artichokes either. It had never seemed like a sacrifice to me to limit our use of these ingredients at home. This is how we smooth down the roughest edges in a relationship. It still came as a surprise, though, to discover that I no longer needed to consider what Eiolf liked or didn't like to eat. The freedom to eat whatever I wanted was not something I had ever been aware of conceding.

I lost a lot of weight without even trying after Eiolf died. Mealtimes came and went, but I wasn't hungry. I think I almost got out of the habit of eating. I was a confident enough cook to dare to try out new recipes when I had people for dinner, but now cooking had become a chore. It was easier not to eat. But of course it wasn't merely my lack of appetite that had led to this sorry state of affairs; I had also lost my appetite for life.

Before, I had prided myself on being able to rustle up a tasty meal in next to no time once we both got home from work. We were a good team in the kitchen, Eiolf and I, working happily side by side. We each had our own particular tasks and areas of responsibility, refined over many years together. That was part of the secret. But half the pleasure of cooking lies in seeking out top-quality raw ingredients together and, not least, in the social aspect of sharing a meal with the one person with whom you would happily be marooned on a desert island. The planning of a meal also gives a thrill of anticipation and quickens the appetite. At the weekends, when we had more time, we would devise more elaborate dinners and invite great and small to come and eat with us. I believe this was one of our trademarks. Now, though, I almost had to force myself to eat, simply to get the nourishment I knew I needed. I hit rock bottom on the evening when I found myself sitting in front of the television, mechanically and apathetically shovelling in mackerel in tomato sauce straight from the can.

One of the main reasons I got into mushrooms was that I liked eating them. I had always thought mushrooms tasted good and not like anything else, but I was amazed to find that many species have their own unique flavour. Some can be extremely subtle, others are simply peculiar and only for specialist palates. I learned early on that it's a good idea to fry different types of mushroom separately. That way you can find out which ones you like best. Because the fact is that mushrooms don't all taste the same, nor do they only smack of earth, leaves, and moss, as wine connoisseurs would have it. I was surprised to learn that the various species each have their own different and distinct texture when cooked: the St George's mushroom keeps its shape well and becomes almost springy, the Orange Birch Bolete is smooth and juicy, and the Shaggy Ink Cap, *Coprinus comatus*, is delicate, light, and silky soft.

Even if the mushroom you have found happens to be a five-star edible species, this doesn't mean it should end up in the frying pan. Some edible mushrooms may also be too old or too worm-eaten to eat. I have spent a lot of time recently with a keen novice mushroomer and have been surprised by how reluctant he is to throw away rotten edible specimens. He doesn't seem to see that they've become inedible. Mushroomers are split on the question of how wormy a mushroom has to be before it ought to be thrown away: some don't mind a few little worms and will joke about the extra protein they provide, others are more choosy. A mushroomer's 'worm limit' is defined by how much of a mushroom they will cut away before they consider it fit to eat. My novice friend is so pleased when he finds an edible mushroom that he is quite prepared to eat every bit of it, no matter how old or wormy it may be. I'm not entirely sure, but I don't think I was quite so undiscriminating when I was a beginner, although there's no doubt that I have become more fussy over the years. I used to bother more about not discarding good edible specimens. These days I know that I'll always find other ones, possibly in better condition, and I'm ruthless when it comes to cutting away inedible parts of my mushrooms.

In Norway, the most common way of cooking mushrooms is to fry them in butter with salt and pepper. The frying pan is heated, a knob of butter added, and once this has melted, the mushrooms are dropped in. One of the first things I learned on the mushrooms for beginners course was that it really ought to be done the other way round: the mushrooms should be sautéed first, in a dry pan over a moderate heat, and only after the liquid from them has evaporated should the butter be added. Mushrooms contain a lot of water, especially if they are picked after several days of rain, so by allowing the liquid to evaporate first you prevent the mushrooms from 'boiling' in the butter and water. As a result, the flavour will be more concentrated. If you're feeling extravagant, you could add some bacon, cream, and/or a dash of sherry along with the salt and pepper. If you have a lot of mushrooms, they also make an excellent accompaniment to steak. If you only have a few, mushrooms on toast is the perfect comfort snack. I think that mushrooms cooked in this fashion taste excellent, but as a Malaysian I know that there are all sorts of other ways of cooking mushrooms which don't involve butter, cream, or sherry — ingredients seldom found in ordinary Asian kitchens. I thought it would be interesting, therefore, to explore other ways of preparing mushrooms. I was also intrigued by the standard notion that mushrooms can never be anything but a dinner-time side-dish. Was there any way they might form the main ingredient in a starter, main course, or even a dessert?

Soup

It doesn't take long to make soup from scratch. It basically makes itself. If I have a lot to do, I'll often take care of the first stage in the morning and finish the soup just before serving. It takes no time to chop an onion and a clove or two of garlic before your breakfast porridge, then at least that's that bit done. This is the base of most of my soups, mushroom or otherwise.

Mushroom soup made with wild mushrooms is something I always recommend to anyone who has only ever tasted the packet soup variety. The difference in taste between wild and shop-bought mushrooms is due to their growth substratum. Shop-bought mushrooms are grown on a mix of fermented horse dung and straw, so it goes without saying that there are limits to how good they can taste. Wild mushrooms start to crop up on lawns as early as the middle of summer. As well as tasting brilliant — one tiny bite will fill the mouth with a lovely nutty flavour — these lawn mushrooms are great because you can pick them on the way home from work. You don't have to change into your foraging gear and make a long foray into the forest. Urban mushrooms are also a good plan B during a long dry spell, when the woods have little to offer, but park lawns and grassy areas in graveyards — which are usually regularly watered by strategically placed sprinklers — more or less guarantee that there will always be some good pickings to be had. Although this does, of course, presuppose that you have one or more nearby mushroom-friendly parks — or graveyards — to nip into.

The challenge with picking mushrooms from grassy lawns lies in not picking the poisonous Yellow-staining Mushroom, *Agaricus xanthodermus*, by mistake, so first you have to learn to identify it. At one of the Norwegian capital's smartest garden parties, as glasses chinked and gossip buzzed, my eye was caught by something else entirely: a Yellow-stainer! I wasn't actually looking for mushrooms, but I suppose this was proof that I did so without even thinking about it. That may well have been the moment when I made the shift from amateur mushroomer to hopeless mushroom freak. Or had that already happened?

According to Norwegian mushroom guides, the Salty Mushroom, *Agaricus bernardii*, has a pungent odour of chicory, radish, and fish, and a slightly bitter taste. This didn't sound like something I would want to put in the pot, but then I discovered that Americans relish this mushroom and never mention it smelling fishy. I have since picked some young

Salty Mushrooms and have to say that they tasted good, even if the flavour could not be described as 'mild', the standard accolade in Norway. I would have no qualms about adding a couple of Salty Mushrooms to a pot of mushroom soup to jazz it up.

Shaggy Ink Cap soup, made from mushrooms picked from your own garden, is a very different kettle of fish, so to speak. The Shaggy Ink Cap is the only mushroom which has to be popped straight into a plastic bag when picked. It has to be kept moist, otherwise the process which causes the mushroom to 'melt' is speeded up and it will turn into a black inky mass. I once came across a large clump of Shaggy Ink Caps when I didn't have a plastic bag on me. What was I to do? Luckily I was out foraging with my first mushroom teacher. He picked some large leaves, about the size of a dinner plate, and we wrapped the mushrooms in these. He also reminded me that the Shaggy Ink Cap must on no account be confused with the Common Ink Cap, *Coprinopsis atramentaria*. The Common Ink Cap can have a similar effect to anti-alcohol drugs like Disulfiram, causing nausea and vomiting, among other unpleasant effects, if mixed with alcohol.

The Shaggy Ink Cap, on the other hand, is a delicate mushroom worth including in a more sophisticated dinner menu. For the soup, steam the Shaggy Ink Caps you have managed to find in a covered pan over a low heat, adding enough chicken stock to cover and a dash of vermouth towards the end. Just before serving, whip an egg yolk and stir this into the soup. If you have any pickled ramson buds or diced pumpkin these can be used as garnish and to offset the richness of the soup.

Later in the season it is the turn of Funnel chanterelle soup. To the base of gently fried onions and garlic, add the chanterelles. After frying these together, add enough stock so that everyone will have a good bowlful. Let the soup simmer a bit and, just before serving, add a dash of cream and sherry. This soup can look rather dark due to the deep-brown hue of the Funnel chanterelles so you might want to try adding a little grated carrot to brighten it up. If a more robust soup is called for, Funnel chanterelles can also cope with the addition of blue cheese and sherry.

A nice, hearty soup can be made from red lentils and dried mushrooms. I made this one day when I didn't have much in the way of fresh ingredients in the house, but found a bag of red lentils at the very back of the cupboard. Again, start with the soup base of chopped onions and garlic. All you need are a handful of lentils, a few dried mushrooms, and a vegetable stock cube. If you want a smoother consistency, all you have to do is blend the soup with the hand blender when it's finished. Add a dollop of sour cream and some finely chopped herbs and you have a simple dish that is both tasty and nourishing.

Coprinus comatus, Shaggy Ink Caps

Mushroom bacon

To make bacon from shiitake mushrooms, start by soaking them in water for about an hour. Squeeze the water out of the mushrooms and slice them into strips. Mix the shiitake strips in a bowl with some olive oil and coarsely ground salt. Heat the oven to 175°C. Spread the shiitakes out on a baking tray and bake for an hour. Stir the mushroom strips about every now and again. Doing them in this way intensifies the flavour of the dried shiitakes, turning them into little taste bombs — a sure-fire hit with vegetarians and others. Mushroom bacon can be eaten as it is, but it can also be used in other ways. Try sprinkling it over soups or salads, for example.

Shiitake mushrooms have long been popular in Asia, where they are widely grown. In China, Japan, and Korea the shiitake has been known and used since prehistoric times. The cultivation method used in China was first described during the Sung dynasty (960–1279). In Asia different classes of dried shiitake are available, from the plumpest, most perfect whole specimens to uneven slices to shiitake dust. In Malaysia, shiitakes are a delicacy to be ordered in posh restaurants. They are not exactly the cheapest item on the menu; the opposite, in fact. So there are usually a few remarks about the number and size of the shiitakes in a dish when it arrives from the kitchen. If your host for the evening is feeling particularly generous you might even be treated to an extra large portion of shiitakes. Many people in Asia also believe that this mushroom has many health benefits. It is regarded as an elixir for long life and is frequently prescribed as a medicine for certain ailments. Compared to other mushrooms, the shiitake generates relatively high levels of Vitamin D, although all mushrooms produce Vitamin D when exposed to UVB rays. Today, shiitake mushrooms are grown not only in Asia, but in Brazil, Russia, and the United States as well. The commercial market for shiitakes is large and still expanding. Originally they were cultivated on tree trunks, but over the past ten years — since growers started using sacks of sawdust — production in the US has increased dramatically. The latter method ensures a shorter cultivation cycle and year-round production of shiitakes. Nowadays you can even buy a little kit and grow shiitake at home in your own kitchen.

Another idea is to make jerky from oyster mushrooms. Normally, jerky — a popular outdoor snack in the United States — consists of strips or chunks of dried, cured, and seasoned meats. To make a vegetarian jerky with oyster mushrooms, the strips of mushroom should first be marinaded in soy sauce, maple syrup, apple cider vinegar, olive oil, ground paprika, and salt. Spread the strips out on a baking tray and bake at 120°C for (approx.) one to two hours, stirring them occasionally. Oyster mushroom jerky tastes slightly sweet and spicy. Once you start eating it, it's hard to stop.

Roasted mushrooms with sesame oil and soy sauce

A guaranteed winner as a starter, and one which is both simple and delicious, is roasted mushrooms. Asian condiments such as sesame oil (a teaspoon) and soy sauce (a tablespoon) are mixed together with chopped garlic and parsley. If you have mushroom soy sauce, use this instead of normal soy sauce. Shop-bought mushrooms or rehydrated shiitakes would work well in this recipe. Remove the mushroom stems and place the mushrooms upside down on a baking tray, (so you can see the gills). Place a teaspoon of the sesame/soy mix onto each mushroom and put the mushrooms into the oven at 125°C for about twenty minutes. The flavour is very intense. These mushrooms are also good as part of a tapas buffet.

Pâté

One of the great things about a pâté is that it can be made well in advance. The classic way of serving it is, of course, as a starter, with toast or crusty bread, but it is also excellent for sandwiches, picnics, or informal lunches — as an elegant alternative or addition to the usual cold cuts, cheese, and so on. And this one can also be served to vegetarians.

For a mushroom pâté, you can use a mixture of fresh and rehydrated mushrooms. You will also need some shallots, a handful of whole almonds, sherry, white miso paste (available from Japanese or other Asian supermarkets), and the liquid in which the rehydrated mushrooms have been steeped. First, roast the almonds in a dry pan until the aroma starts to come through. Be careful not to let them burn. Remove and set aside. Then heat the oil in the pan and fry the mushrooms. Add the miso paste and the steeping liquid. Start with one tablespoon of miso. Fry over a low heat until all the liquid has evaporated. Add the sherry and remove the pan from the heat. Heat some oil in another pan and fry the shallots over a low heat. Stir the cooked shallots into the mushroom mixture and blend with a hand blender. Season with salt and pepper and possibly a little more miso. Your pâté is now ready. Just set it in the fridge until half an hour before serving. This pâté could also be served as a main course.

Pickled mushrooms

Pickling is a good way of using up any leftover mushrooms, especially if they are nice small specimens. Pickled mushrooms can form an accompaniment to many main dishes, their piquancy acting as an excellent foil for the richness of butter and cream-based sauces. Fry wild mushrooms such as Penny Buns and chanterelles in a dry and moderately hot pan to release the liquid from the mushrooms. Add finely chopped shallots and a little oil. Make a vinaigrette from one part balsamic vinegar to three parts olive oil. Pour this over the mushroom mixture. Season with salt, spices, or herbs. Spoon the whole lot into a clean jar and leave to stand in the fridge for at least 24 hours. Before serving sprinkle generously with shavings of Parmesan or Swedish *västerbottenost*.

Mushroom roast

If you are thinking of serving mushrooms as a main dish, a mushroom roast might be the way to go. It's always a good idea to start by preheating the oven, in this case to 160°C, and lining a baking tin with baking parchment. Warm a tablespoon of olive oil and 15 grams of butter in a pan and gently fry one onion and two celery stalks (finely chopped) for about five minutes. Add two cloves of garlic (finely chopped) and 200 grams of fresh mushrooms (sliced) and continue frying for about 10 minutes. Now add a bell pepper (finely chopped) and one carrot (grated). Fry for another three minutes or so, then stir in one teaspoon each of oregano and smoked paprika. Now it's time to add body to your roast with 100 grams of red lentils, two tablespoons of tomato puree, and 300 millilitres of vegetable stock. Allow to simmer on a low heat until all of the liquid has been absorbed and the mixture is fairly dry. Set the pan aside and leave to cool. Finally, add 100 grams of breadcrumbs, 150 grams of mixed nuts (roughly chopped), three large eggs (lightly whisked), 100 grams of cheese (preferably a well-matured one such as Parmesan or similar), a handful of chopped parsley, salt, and pepper. Mix well and transfer to the baking tin. Cover with tin foil and bake in the oven for 20 minutes. Then remove the tinfoil and bake for another 10 to 15 minutes, until the roast feels firm to the touch. Leave to cool and serve.

Mushroom sauce

I recently served a very successful slow-roasted veal with mushroom sauce. The veal was good, but it was the sauce that made it something to write home about. My guest ended up taking an extra helping of the meat just to have more of the sauce.

Start by soaking as many dried mushrooms as you can spare for a sauce in the pan used to brown the veal (lamb or beef would also work). Using the same pan means that any last juices or meat scrapings from the browning will go straight into the sauce. Set the pan on the hob and turn on the heat low. Add veal or other stock and the mushrooms. After these have simmered for around ten minutes, it's the turn of the dairy products, like butter and cream, to round the whole thing off. Because I had duck fat in the fridge, and fat of some sort is the basis of all good sauces, I used that instead of butter. I used a hand blender to puree the chunks of mushroom into a smooth sauce. There is no need, here, to thicken with flour, since the mushrooms do that job themselves. As a final touch, I stirred in a tablespoon of good mustard. I used neither shallots nor alcohol of any sort in the sauce, but one could certainly do so. Just before serving I also added a good grinding of pink pepper.

Candy Caps

Cut into the gills of a milk cap mushroom and they will exude a milky fluid. In Norway, many people recognise edible milk caps when they see them growing under pine or fir trees because of their orange-coloured milk. These edible milk caps are very popular, both with mushroom pickers and with worms. So it's a matter of getting to the mushrooms before the worms do. There are many different milk caps to be found in Norway. In some cases, the milk turns purple on contact with the air. In others, the milk may be pink, yellow, white, or even clear, as clear as tears. As well as having coloured milk, some of the Norwegian species also have a quite distinct odour.

The Candy Cap, *Lactarius rubidus*, is an aromatic edible milk cap found primarily in the United States. This species grows in small areas along the Californian coast. When dried, the Candy Cap smells of maple syrup, caramel, fennel, and curry. In California, the Candy Cap season starts in January and local mycological societies get off to a good start by arranging special expeditions to find this early mushroom, just as in Norway we have our St George's expeditions around the end of May or beginning of June. In 2012, researchers discovered the source of the Candy Cap's unique aroma: sotolon, an organic compound which, in small amounts, smells of maple syrup, sherry, and caramel and, in larger concentrations, of curry. Run a finger over the cap and you will notice that the surface is slightly nubbly, like the skin of a clementine. This is a good clue to its identification since, in other respects, the Candy Cap is just a nondescript little brown mushroom.

I had long dreamed of getting hold of some Candy Caps and making a dessert with them. A lot of people look surprised when I say this, the received wisdom being that all mushrooms need is a bit of salt and pepper, end of story. To adherents of this school of thought, the idea of using mushrooms in cakes or desserts is inconceivable, but that is only because they don't know any better. Until I moved to Norway I had always associated avocados with dessert: at home in Malaysia I used to eat avocado with palm sugar. Likewise, though oppositely, liquorice is much more than just a flavouring for confectionery. In specialist liquorice shops one can now buy liquorice powder, for example, to sprinkle on a steak. So when I realised that mushrooms could be used in desserts, I had to give it a go.

On the Internet there are plenty of American recipes for and pictures of Candy Cap ice cream, pannacotta, whipped cream, crème brûlée, pancakes, biscuits, and other sweet treats. You don't need to rehydrate the mushrooms. The trick is to crush the dried mushrooms and mix this precious powder with the other dry ingredients. Be careful, though, not to use too many Candy Caps, because they can be rather bitter in taste. 5 grams of Candy Cap is enough for a 23 x 8 cm cheesecake. All the descriptions of Candy Cap desserts which I found said that they did not taste of mushrooms, but of maple syrup. Apparently this flavour can linger on the tongue long into the following day. I couldn't wait to experiment with this rare and fascinating mushroom from California. So I was delighted when I managed to obtain a couple of grams of Candy Cap from the American west coast.

Imagine my disappointment, then, when I discovered later that there are at least two other species of Candy Cap and that one of these, the Curry Milk Cap, *Lactarius camphoratus*, actually grew in Norway. The name Candy Cap appears to be a blanket term for several members of the *Lactarius* family, all of which have an aromatic odour, particularly when dried. While the Californian mushroom smells of maple syrup, the Norwegian variety smells more of curry. There is no tradition in Norway for eating the Curry Milk Cap. It is regarded as inedible. According to the popular Swedish field guide *Sopp i Norden og Europa* by Bo Nylén, the initial taste is mild, but growing sharper. A quick Google search on *L. camphoratus* reveals, however, that this mushroom is eaten in other countries, where it is dried and used as seasoning in soups and sauces. This might well be another example of national differences as to what is considered (in)edible. In the UK, *L. camphoratus* is sold as a cooking ingredient under the name Curry Milk Cap. It is also sold commercially in China. It was annoying to think that I had possibly paid way over the odds for an American relative of an overlooked mushroom that was in plentiful supply at home.

Chanterelle and apricot ice cream with candied chanterelle chunks

I simply had to try this recipe, having had a problem with the apricot aroma of chanterelles ever since I began to take a serious interest in mushrooming.

First candy the chanterelles. For this you will need one cup of sugar and one cup of water together with one cinnamon stick. Bring to the boil and reduce to a syrup. Add two cups of small fresh chanterelles or larger ones sliced thinly or diced. Allow to simmer for 10 minutes. Remove the pan from the heat and take out the cinnamon stick. Strain off the syrup and leave the chanterelles to cool and dry on a sheet of greaseproof paper. And there you have them: candied mushrooms — the perfect secret ingredient to keep in your larder, ready to psyche out your culinary rivals.

While the chanterelles are drying, you can start to make the ice cream. Put milk (one cup), double cream (one cup), and fresh chanterelles (one cup) into a pan, along with sprigs of fresh mint, and warm gently. Alternatively, you could use one-third of a cup of dried chanterelles. Then add five or six chopped, dried apricots. In a separate bowl whisk together half a cup of sugar and two egg yolks. When the milk and cream mixture is just starting to simmer, remove the pan from the heat. Take out the mint and throw away. Slowly pour the mixture from the pan into the bowl containing the whisked sugar and egg yolks, stirring continually. Pour the whole thing back into the pan and warm gently. Add the grated rind of half a lemon. Keep stirring, being careful not to let the mixture burn. Be careful, also, not to let it boil. The mixture will gradually start to thicken. Take off the heat, allow to cool and place in the fridge. After approx. two hours pour the mixture into an ice cream maker to finish off. To serve, garnish with little chunks of candied chanterelle.

'Dogsup'

The composer John Cage not only loved picking mushrooms, he loved cooking with them as well. This is his version of ketchup, or catsup, which he dubbed 'dogsup'.

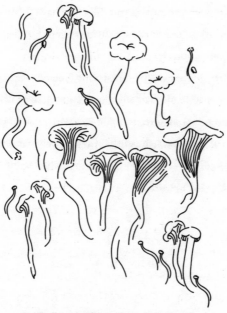

Craterellus tubaeformis, funnel chanterelles

You will need: edible mushrooms, salt, ginger, bay leaves, cayenne pepper, black pepper, mace, allspice and brandy. Finely dice the mushroom caps and slice the stems. Put the mushrooms into a bowl and add one tablespoon of salt for every 500 grams of mushrooms. Leave to stand in a cool place for three days, stirring and turning the mix at regular intervals. On the third day, heat the mixture in a pan for about 30 minutes to draw the last of the liquid from the mushrooms. Strain off the liquid and blend the mushrooms in a food processor. Season the mushroom liquid with some chopped ginger, the mace, bay leaves, black pepper, allspice, and a dash of cayenne pepper. Blend the mushrooms and the liquid together and cook until reduced by half. Add a tablespoon of brandy.

When I came across Cage's recipe it made me think of the 'mushroom soy sauce' which some Norwegian mushroomers make and use as an alternative to soy sauce. Cage preferred a thicker consistency, so he didn't discard the mushrooms after straining off the liquid. Both versions are great for adding a little oomph to a dish.

The bathroom scales

I regained the weight I had lost after Eiolf died. I wasn't too happy about this at first, but then it occurred to me that it was probably a good sign: the bathroom scales were signalling, loud and clear, that I was making my way back to my old weight ... and to life.

Divorce vs. death

After Eiolf's death, I had many a heart-to-heart with a woman friend who was facing up to the fact that her marriage was over. She told me, in heartrending terms, about the last evening before she moved out of the house, and how she had gone from room to room, saying goodbye. She must have felt as if she was being thrown out of the family home that she had helped to create over so many years. I don't know much about divorce, but my friend and I discovered many points in common in our respective wanderings in the wilderness. And many dissimilarities. Is it possible to compare and measure different experiences of loss? Is it worse to be divorced than widowed? In a divorce there are at least two parties, so there can be feelings of resentment and humiliation, shame and/or guilt. My friend also had to accept that her ex-husband had his own conflicting narrative of how things had been between them and where it had all gone wrong.

'It might be easier if he was dead,' she whispered.

Latin class

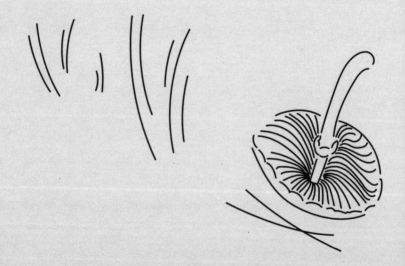

As a newcomer to the mushroom community I was overwhelmed by how much there was to learn. I took pictures of the mushrooms I learned to recognise, consulted books and the Internet, and spoke to veteran mushroom pickers. How did the experts manage to identify so many species? What was it they looked for, what particular features? There is no official contest to decide who is top mushroomer, but anyone able to identify a fungus that has defeated everyone else soon earns respect. I was greatly impressed by how much my fellow foragers knew and felt that I was surrounded by giants. Those mushroomers who knew all the scientific names had a way of casually rattling them off, *en passant*, which immediately raised their standing in the knowledge hierarchy — in my eyes and, I believe, in the eyes of others. I breathed a sigh of relief when I heard that the mushroom inspector's exam confined itself to the Norwegian common names. I would never have been able to learn all of the scientific names in Latin and/ or Greek along with everything else (the Latin names are often derived from the Greek). To begin with, therefore, it was a mystery to me why people spent time and energy on learning them.

Since then I have come to realise that there can be many good reasons for familiarising oneself with the scientific names of mushrooms. If, for example, you think you have identified a species correctly, but decide to google the common name in your own particular country, just to double-check, you will get some few hits. But if you key in the scientific name you will get many, many more hits — and just as many more pictures. Each country has its own common name (or names) for mushrooms. Even within Scandinavia they can vary: common Norwegian names won't necessarily get you very far in Sweden or Denmark. The mushroom which is known in the UK as the Penny Bun, goes by the name of King Bolete in the United States, cèpe in France, and porcini in Italy. The Penny Bun's scientific name is *Boletus edulis*, an appellation unique to this species. In order to communicate with fellow mushroomers on social media or take part in international events, a knowledge of the scientific names is essential: a mastery of mushroom Latin is not merely an affectation.

You can, of course, just memorise all the scientific names without knowing what they mean, but it's more fun if you know what they refer to. Every piece of mycological information contributes to the understanding of each mushroom, but the name has a key part to play. It often provides an important clue to a fungus' distinguishing features. The young Wood Blewit mushroom, for example, is certainly a lilacky blue, but young or old, its scientific name, *Lepista nuda*, perfectly describes the surface of its cap. The Latin word *nuda* is the feminine form of *nudus*,

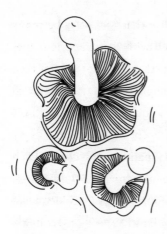

Lepista nuda, Wood Blewit

meaning bare or naked, and the Wood Blewit's cap both looks and feels like naked skin. From this same root come the words 'nude' and 'nudist'. Mushroom Latin is also a good way of learning more about words and their history.

The Wood Blewit mushroom can often be found growing in fairy rings. With its blueish tinge it looks like something one could only find in an enchanted wood. In fact, it grows in perfectly ordinary forests and on garden lawns. Wood Blewits have their loyal fans, who happily go to all the bother of blanching them — i.e. bringing them to the boil, then draining them — before frying them. I have followed this somewhat laborious process and sampled the result, but decided that the Wood Blewit mushroom was not for me. This conclusion may, however, have been coloured by my first mushroom teacher's description of *Lepista nuda*: that it smells of burnt rubber and tastes like kidneys. I have since learned that the Wood Blewit mushroom which grows in beechwoods tastes excellent, unlike its fellows which grow under the silver fir. So the last word on this matter has not yet been said. But when I come upon a Wood Blewit the pleasure is always threefold. First I feel happy to have found a mushroom which, until recently, I didn't even know existed. Then I pick it, as a surprise for a friend who loves Wood Blewit mushrooms. And lastly I nod and smile to myself at its splendid scientific name.

Idiot's guide to mushroom Latin

Learning mushroom Latin is not as difficult as you might think. Obviously it helps to have a good and patient teacher. I have had a great many conversations with mushroom expert and Latin scholar Oliver Smith, who has given me a whole new insight into the hidden world of scientific classification. The taxonomical terms 'family' and 'genus' are not, as some might think, interchangeable. My study of mushrooms has taught me that in biology it is important to differentiate between these two terms, each of which designates a different rank in the taxonomic hierarchy. Sometimes I forget myself and refer somewhat imprecisely to 'types' of mushroom, or confuse the different ranks in the biological family tree. Such inaccuracy can cause some mushroom experts to roll their eyes. On the other hand, you may be lucky enough to encounter patient veterans who will talk you through this biology lesson one more time.

When research into this field was in its infancy, scientists were dependent on macroscopic observations, i.e. what can be seen with the naked eye. This was followed by the microscopical study of mushroom spores, the idea here being that the spores are like individual, unique 'fingerprints'. In actual fact, however, it is not necessarily easy to identify a species with absolute certainty, even with a very strong microscope. Here, too, experience and informed guesswork play a large part. Since the introduction of Scanning electron microscopy (SEM) and DNA analysis, there has been a rapid increase in changes in species classification. The same goes for the attendant scientific names. One woman friend, who has been gathering mushrooms all her life, told me about what she referred to in Norwegian as *vårmusseronger*, a nice and rather droll name, I thought. The problem was, though, that I couldn't find any mention of these in my mushroom guides. Eventually it dawned on me that *vårmusserong* was the old name for what is now known as the *vårfagerhatt* — *Calocybe gambosa*. The reason for the confusion is that this species used to be known as *Tricholoma gambosa*, but was later renamed. These things happen, even in the best modern families: new members arrive, old ones leave, genus names change, and sometimes so too do species names. Interestingly, though, the St George's mushroom appears always to have gone by this name, whatever its Latin label.

The unique status of each species is ensured by the rules governing their naming, as laid down by the International Code of Botanical Nomenclature (ICN). There are two parts to a scientific name: first the generic name, then the specific name or epithet. Together the generic name and the epithet constitute the mushroom's full scientific or species name. Both should be written in italics. I always think of the generic name as the mushroom's surname and the epithet as its first name. This makes perfect sense to me, born as I was into the Chinese tradition, whereby the surname comes first. The initial letter of the generic name is always capitalised. The epithet can refer to any of a species' salient characteristics, be it colour, form, smell, taste, size, or something else entirely.

Colour and form

Reference to colour in a name usually pertains to the appearance of the cap and the stem, but may also be inspired by the gills, the spore dust, or even a mushroom's 'milk'. The scientific name for the Blackening Russula, for example, is *Russula nigricans*. It is a member of the *Russula* genus. Its specific name *nigricans*, derives from *niger*, the Latin for black. In this case, both the mushroom's common name and its scientific name refer to its colour. Young specimens are a dirty olive-brown, old ones soot-black, and the mature spring mushroom has a charred look to it. It is a sturdy, fleshy, solid mushroom, usually pretty well embedded in the ground.

A quick look through the field guides provides lots of other examples of epithets derived from a mushroom's colour. The Orange Peel Fungus has the scientific name *Aleuria aurantia*. The epithet *aurantia* comes from the Latin word *aurum*, meaning gold. The Orange Peel Fungus is a beautiful little mushroom: with its graceful, sculptural cups, it can be found growing in dense clumps alongside paths all over the countryside. It is edible, but there's not much meat to it, so maybe it is best left to adorn the wayside. Every time I see these mushrooms I find myself wondering whether it would be possible to silver them and make them into ear-rings — their sinuous cup shapes have such a modern look to them. The Copper Spike, or *Chroogomphus rutilus*, takes its specific name from the Latin *rutilus*, meaning red, reddish, or red-gold. This mushroom has a firm, plug-like stem. When fried it turns beetroot-red almost immediately, and if you eat a lot of Copper Spikes your urine will be red the next day — which is good to know beforehand. The Copper Spike is a sturdy mushroom with a little boss or umbo in the centre of the cap and I, for one, think it very tasty. Find one Copper Spike and there's a good chance that you'll find more of this mushroom with the distinctive red-gold flesh.

The *venetus* part of the species *Cortinarius venetus*' name means blue-green or sea-blue. Here Oliver Smith reminds me that Venice takes it name from the same Latin root. The interesting thing about this mushroom is that it can be used as a dye. If, for instance, you use it to dye a pair of white woollen socks they will look green in daylight, but under the disco lights they will be luminescent. In fact, though, this mushroom looks neither blue nor sea-green. Instead it is a dull brown colour with a hint of olive-green. So in this case the Norwegian common name for *Cortinarius venetus*, *grønn slørsopp*, meaning literally 'Green Veiled Mushroom', is more apt than the scientific one. Then we have *Laccaria amethystina*, the Amethyst Deceiver, its specific name coming from its colour, the deep violet of the gemstone. For anyone who imagines that mushrooms are only ever white or brown it comes as quite a surprise to see the Amethyst Deceiver for the first time. Every part of this little fungus is violet: cap, gills, stem, and, as you will see if you slice into it, flesh. It is another of those species which looks as if it would be more at home in an enchanted forest than in a plain, solid pinewood.

The Bloody Milk Cap, *Lactarius sanguifluus*, is a salmon-pink mushroom with blood-red milk. Hence its epithet, from *sanguis*, the Latin for blood. The French term for a rare steak, *saignant*, comes from the same root. I have seen big baskets of Bloody Milk Caps in markets in Spain, where it is considered a delicacy. In these markets they are also often arranged in little pyramids, something which always makes me think of the pickers, the work, and the logistics behind it. It's so nice to see wild mushrooms on sale in shops and on market stalls abroad, where the variety of different species on offer and their quality are a clear sign that customers there are much more discerning than in Norway, for example. I'm sorry to say that in this country I have seen chanterelles and other woodland mushrooms on sale in trendy greengrocers' shops at exorbitant prices and of such poor quality that they were fit only for the bin. The milk of edible Norwegian milk caps is more of a carroty red, and it pours out if you as much as nick the gills with the edge of a knife. The inedible Bloody Brittlegill or *Russula sanguinea* has a bright red cap. The stem is firm, it has a fruity smell, and the taste — if you dare to try it, which I have never done — is hot and peppery and slightly bitter.

One of the most sensational stories told in my local society

Sarcosoma globosum,
Witches' Cauldron

concerns a mushroom which was thought to have been extinct for over 70 years, but which was rediscovered in 2009. This resurrected fungus was the Witches' Cauldron, *Sarcosoma globosum*, and its discovery brought people flocking to the spot where it had been found, in Ringerike, north-west of Oslo; an almost sacred journey which mushroom enthusiasts still make to this day. To an outsider, the Witches' Cauldron looks like a disgusting, dark, gelatinous lump. I was fortunate enough to be invited along on a pilgrimage to Ringerike with some nice senior mushroomers. I was the only person in the group who had never seen this centrefold fungus. The others simply had the urge to see the wonder again. The fact that the Witches' Cauldron is inedible was of no matter as far as my fellow pilgrims were concerned.

Hardcore mushroomers are always hungry for knowledge. They are not only interested in gathering edible mushrooms; they have a deep desire to learn more about *all* fungi. Some seem to feel that devoting time and energy to the service of mushrooming is the be-all and end-all in life. To them, there is something slightly vulgar about being interested in mushrooms only as food. It took me a little while to realise that asking whether a mushroom is edible or not means risking being labelled as just another 'chanterelle-ist'. I have certainly learned to be quite careful about asking this question when I'm with some of the real hardliners. Although I love eating mushrooms I am also a serious mushroom gatherer and now I was on my way to see the Witches' Cauldron for myself.

We followed the local guide into Ringerike Forest. The Witches' Cauldron appears in the spring. Its plump cup shape and blackish hue seem almost perfectly designed by Nature to catch the first rays of sunlight.

The trilling of the birds proclaimed that May was upon us; the air smelled faintly of sap and springtime, but I'm not sure if anyone noticed. Nor do I think anyone noticed the nettles in the ditches, shooting up, all abristle, to greet the spring, and just tall enough to be picked for a lovely nettle and lovage soup, garnished with a poached egg. Not to mention the caraway growing nearby, the much sought-after young, pale-green rosettes of the caraway used by those in the know in their Constitution Day soup, no less. Having followed in the footsteps of the experts in The Greater Oslo Fungi and Useful Plants Society, I now knew what people meant when they described the forest as a treasure-house. Those tender shoots that I had previously dismissed as rabbit food were now precious and nutritious food for the table, to be picked during those brief, intense weeks of spring. In the heart of Ringerike Forest everyone was respectfully silent and very focused. For my own part I was quivering with suspense.

I didn't see the Witches' Cauldrons at first, but then our guide pointed to a large, round, dark lump at the foot of a tree. And lo and behold, there they were. Not just one, but a whole clutch of Witches' Cauldrons, all different sizes, shapes, and ages. Most were about the size of an orange and they seemed to be filled with a sort of glutinous substance which was encased within a black, leathery shell. The tops of the mushrooms quivered slightly, like half-set jelly. It was the weirdest thing I had ever seen.

Epithets may also be inspired by a mushroom's shape. The Witches' Cauldron is spherical in shape, hence *globosum*, meaning sphere- or globe-shaped. It can be as big as a tennis ball, but usually weighs only a couple of hundred grams more. I've heard of children in Sweden, where this mushroom is more common, throwing them at each other like sooty snowballs, although when the Witches' Cauldrons split and the black, gluey contents spurt out, making a terrible mess, this may not seem quite so amusing or be as well-received at home. Some Swedish bakers even make chocolate fondants in the shape of Witches' Cauldrons. These must surely be worth a trip to Sweden for every mushroom and/or chocolate fan.

The White Webcap, *Leucocortinarius bulbiger*, has a strange bulbous stipe. The Latin word bulbus means 'onion-shaped' — a perfect description of this mushroom's stem base. Even more graphically *à propos* is the Norwegian common name for the White Webcap: *klumpfotsoppen* — literally 'club-foot mushroom'. I had never seen this very rare mushroom with the strange foot. The Greek word for foot is *pous*. In the specific names of mushrooms this often becomes *pus*. Thus the scientific name of the beautiful, though, acrid tasting Bitter Beech Bolete is *Boletus calopus*: *calo* meaning 'beautiful' and *'pus'* meaning foot. If you have ever seen a Bitter Beech Bolete, you will understand how it came by this name. And the red stem, covered in a rough mesh pattern, is unmistakeable.

Oliver Smith turned up for one of our Latin sessions with an old rucksack out of which, slowly and with a great flourish, he produced a freeze-dried Freckled Dapperling, *Echinoderma asperum*. He twirled it gently between his fingers, not saying a word. It was a little diminished due to the freeze-drying, but the warty, dark-brown scales on its cap were still clearly discernible. *Aspera* is the Latin for 'rough'. Smith twirled the mushroom and asked me to note how pale the gills were. This was a clear sign that this could *not* be a Prince mushroom, with which the Dapperling might otherwise be confused: a dangerous mistake that he had seen others make. The Prince mushroom has a princely flavour, while *Echinoderma asperum* is not for human consumption. Both mushrooms have small brown scales on their caps, but there the likeness ends.

Odour, aroma, and size

In addition to shape and colour, a mushroom's epithet can be an indication of its odour and aroma. The Aniseed Funnel Mushroom, *Clitocybe odora*, smells so strongly and clearly of aniseed that I have heard of people soaking this blue-green fungus in alcohol in hopes of producing a good tipple. The Latin word *odor* means smell or fragrance, so it is hardly surprising that *Russula odorata* should have a distinct scent, as everyone who has smelled this mushroom can attest to. It has a fruity, aromatic odour.

Many epithets refer to the size of a mushroom. So, for example, the scientific name of the Tiny Earthstar is *Geastrum minimum* — the Latin word *minimus* meaning smallest. The first time I saw the Tiny Earthstar what immediately sprang to mind were Christmas decorations. As its name suggests, this mushroom has a distinct star shape. It is actually quite surprising that no one has thought of spraying them with gold paint and selling them at extortionate prices in fancy home interiors shops. At the other end of the scale, we have the Giant Puffball, *Calvatia gigantea*. *Gigantem* meaning, of course, gigantic or very large. The Giant Puffball is a very white, very round mushroom which no child can resist kicking. When it reaches maturity it explodes, releasing clouds of mature spores. But if you find one which is perfectly white inside it can be cut into slices, dipped in egg and breadcrumbs and fried. Giant Puffballs can grow to the size of pumpkins and need to be secured with the car seatbelt before being transported straight home to the kitchen. On one occasion I was invited to join a select little group from my local society on an expedition to the island of Bjerkøya in Oslo Fjord. The purpose of this trip was to find the Giant Knight, *Tricholoma colossus*, a very rare mushroom which is also red-listed. Its epithet, *colossus* says it all. After a long search we eventually found one solitary specimen at the top of a long, winding, and, at times, very steep path through the sparse pinewood. The cap of the Giant Knight, which is round, firm, and compact, can be as much as 25 centimetres in width.

Macrolepiota procera, Parasol Mushroom

Another large, but not so uncommon, mushroom is the Parasol Mushroom, *Macrolepiota procera*. The Parasol is easily recognisable, not least because it is tall and slender and upright, as the word *procera* (meaning long, high or lofty), indicates. It has never been found in Oslo itself, but is more common on the west side of Oslo Fjord. I found it for the first time outside of Norway, on a beach on the French island of Corsica. It was the last day of a mycology conference and we had a little free time before the gala dinner. Evening was drawing on, but the Mediterranean sun was still shining. The beach was more or less deserted apart from a runner or two. The running craze had obviously reached Corsica, best known for its farming and fishing — and as the birthplace of

Napoleon. Were these runners yet another sign of the mainland prosperity flowing across the Ligurian Sea to Corsica?

This was just the sort of question that Eiolf would have had something to say about. Since his death, every time I am on a plane I gaze out of the windows at the clouds. I know it's completely irrational, but I am actually looking for him, this man who believed neither in Heaven nor Hell.

On the programme for the first evening of the conference was a talk on mushrooms that grow among sand dunes. Sand mushrooms on Corsica were clearly nothing like the Norwegian *sandsopp* (literally 'sand mushroom'), *Suillus variegatus*, known in English as the Velvet Bolete. The latter grows primarily in nutrient-poor coniferous forests, far from the sea. I had not yet had a chance to explore the Corsican beaches properly, but I was secretly hoping to find mushrooms in the sand before we left the island. We had worked out that our best bet was to check out spots scattered with seaweed, kelp, and Mediterranean succulents — downy plants like cacti, but without the spines: the mushrooms had to draw sustenance from something. To begin with all we found were some strange-looking beach plants that none of us recognised. Then suddenly I spotted a large Parasol Mushroom.

The sight of it hit me right in the solar plexus. The stem of this mushroom can be up to 40 centimetres tall and the cap as much as 30 centimetres in diameter. The stem has a distinctive zig-zag, snakeskin pattern and there is a double ring around the stem which can be slid up and down. The Parasol is a very popular edible mushroom. I had heard that it could be fried like steak or dipped in egg and breadcrumbs and then fried. It is also a favourite with vegetarians. I almost jumped for joy. We dropped down onto the succulents — which were well able to take our collective weight — to photograph our find from every possible angle. The rays of setting sun were still so strong that one of our party had to stand in front of them and act as a screen for our photoshoot. We all knew that if you find one mushroom, the odds are that there will be another close by. And we were right: not far off we found a colony of Fly Agaric. On a beach on Corsica. The Fly Agarics clearly didn't need birch trees with which to form mycorrhizal relationships. A nearby willow tree would serve just as well.

The gift that goes on giving

As we have seen, a knowledge of the scientific names of mushrooms is essential if you wish to converse with mushroom nerds in other parts of the world. So mushroom Latin is not just some single-use, throwaway resource, it is a gift that goes on giving.

It reminds me of one time when I had dinner at a friend's house. After dinner he let me hear some of his favourite numbers from his Spotify playlist. This was a few years after Eiolf died. My music-loving friend played these tracks one after the other like a DJ high on illegal substances. I was so inspired by his enthusiasm for the music that when I got home I logged on to my own Spotify account, which had languished, forgotten, since Eiolf died.

I started to shake and my cheeks started to burn when I saw that Eiolf and I had shared our playlists just before he died, although I had no memory of this.

All at once I had hours of music that Eiolf had chosen and carefully compiled. I obviously hadn't listened to this playlist before because there were a number of unexpected choices, numbers which were new to me. It was good to be able to listen afresh to certain songs, but it was also simply glorious to enjoy the playlist in its entirety. What these artists and the songs had in common was that they had spoken to Eiolf. I almost had palpitations when I realised what a tremendous gift I had been given. I had to listen to Eiolf's playlist a little at a time to let the music sink in.

I pressed 'Play' and gave thanks for this blessing.

A kiss
from heaven

Never be afraid to venture outside your comfort zone. That was just one of the important lessons on fieldwork I learned from my anthropology teacher, Professor Fredrik Barth. There is always a temptation, when on foreign ground, to simply carry on talking to the first helpful informant you encounter. Barth's point was that I should always endeavour to speak to people I hadn't met before and visit places I hadn't been before, constantly expanding my body of data. The anthropologist is thereby forced to arrive at more valid and cogent conclusions.

In many ways this was also the approach I took in my fieldwork of the heart. Hard though it was to be lost and wandering through desolate and unknown territory, I can see now that, strange as it might seem, it was a good thing that I didn't find my way again straight off. Sometimes it can even come as an unexpected pleasure not to know where you are. This presupposes, though, that you can stand the torture of not knowing.

To keep expanding your comfort zone is not a bad strategy when you are searching for new meaning.

For a long time I thought it was just a coincidence that mushrooms, of all things, should have been the saving of me. But when I took up mushroom gathering I still wasn't really capable of mixing with other people. So maybe I was better off with only hushed woods and mute mushrooms for company? Not until I had emerged from the tunnel of grief was I ready for other forms of recreation. So, on reflection, maybe it wasn't that much of a coincidence after all.

Mushrooms have changed my life. When I go mushrooming I am looking for food, but I'm also pleased to find inedible, but mycologically interesting fungi. And a trip to a new mushroom site with a new mushroom buddy simply adds to the experience.

On a ramble through the fungi kingdom, the senses have to be switched on, the mind tuned in. I sense something new, therefore I am a new person.

Foraging gives me a feeling of flow — 'mushroom flow', that is what I am hunting for, that sense of being one with nature. I hunt to survive and to live. To feel the flow is to find meaning, and to find meaning is to quiet and transform the storm inside.

Looking back on it, I can see that my journey through the landscape of grief gradually turned into a progress towards a new spring. Through my outer and inner journeys, life came creeping back and I had the unwonted feeling of seeing myself anew.

'Come to Valka with us. Sturm und Drang are playing tonight, they used to be Oslo Tangoforening, you know?'

My old university professor came out with this impromptu invitation when I happened to bump into him on the street late one weekday evening. I had just left work; I was mentally drained and had been looking forward to getting home. Nonetheless, he talked me into it.

The Valkyrien restaurant is a an old, low-budget watering hole in Majorstua on the west side of Oslo. Popularly known as 'Valka' or 'Valken' it was established sometime before 1912. I went along and it proved to have been a good decision. I hadn't had so much fun in ages.

The joint was already jumping when we stepped in to the warmth from the street, where the cold bit right to the bone. I had looked into Valkyrien once, just out of curiosity, many years earlier, before the blessing of the smoking ban, but had turned on my heel in the doorway. The air had been thick with cigarette smoke and the bar's patrons had seemed almost to blend in with the grey wallpaper. Not my sort of place.

It was a different story this time. There was the same old jumble of tables and chairs, but they were no longer enveloped in tobacco fumes, and there was a band playing lively gypsy music. There didn't seem to be a free seat in the house. On the walls hung framed photos of Willy Brandt and Lev Trotsky. The customers were a motley mix of diplomats and down-and-outs: I would have had a hard job telling which were which if my professor friend hadn't been there to tell me. The average

age and academic level were high. Latin quotations would not have been met by blank stares here, but there was nothing stuffy or strait-laced about the cheers which greeted particularly popular numbers.

Five musicians, each with a glass close to hand, were playing their hearts out. Were they paid in liquid vitamin B, I wonder? The violinist had come straight from a concert with the Oslo Philharmonic, but the metro ran straight from the Concert Hall in the city centre to Majorstua, so that was no problem. Valka blossomed with all its rough charm. People clapped and boisterously called out their requests to the band. They appeared to know all five members personally. Occasionally the audience would be shushed by a few particularly keen fans, anxious to hear the words of a song or a solo passage. The professor wanted to hear Shostakovich's *Waltz No. 2*, and his wish was granted. After a few subsequent visits to Valka I now know that here you can also have the pleasure of hearing cheerful amateurs, who will take to the stage with their instruments to provide entertainment while Sturm und Drang enjoy their 'half-litre break' or, more often, after the band is finished for the evening.

I surprised myself by staying on that first evening, when all I had really wanted to do was to get home to my bed, but it probably had something to do with my general state of mind. Previously, I had responded to all kind enquiries with a 'Yes, thanks, I'm doing okay' out of habit and politeness, but now I could say it and really mean it. The roller blind had whipped up and daylight had poured in. I needed to get out in the sunlight and hear the grit scrunch under my feet as I walked along a woodland way. Given time the light will penetrate to the darkest corners of despair. There was no doubt in my mind that I was, at long last, telling the truth.

At first it was a physical sensation. The great yoke that had been bearing down on my shoulders, vanished from one moment to the next. The expression 'burdened with grief' was not coined without reason. And at that same instant I felt my spirits lift. It reminded me of the first minutes after a blood transfusion at the hospital. Oxygen seemed to surge and swirl through my veins out of sheer bliss.

In the depths of my distress I had as little sparkle and energy as an old dishrag, but now I had the urge to do a few extra press-ups and add a few more plates to the barbell. Now the birds sang in chorus — wasn't that the robin, I heard, welcoming the break of day? Spring was in the air and the snow was starting to melt. The snowdrops and the winter aconites had made their appearance on the little strips of garden outside the tenement buildings in Fagerborg.

At last my heartbeat and that of the universe were in sync. At last my heart could smile again. Now it was easy to get up and greet a lovely morning. I looked out of the window and saw the world with fresh eyes. I wanted to be a part of that.

Where is Eiolf, now that my grief is not crowding out everything else?

He is an imprint on my heart which I will carry with me all my life.

But I have to admit that I always spare an extra glance for couples — not young people, but those of a more mature vintage — walking by, hand in hand.

Bliss

I've lost my husband, I say, and by this most people understand that my husband is dead. But when I say he's lost what I mean is that I look for him, for signs that he is still a part of life here on Earth, of my life. I have a secret hope that maybe he blows me a kiss now and then or waves to me, in some ingenious way that only he could devise. From the bereavement support group I've learned that even the most dyed-in-the-wool atheists and rationalists can occasionally be prone to the feeling that their loved one is close by. I have had this same feeling myself more than once. I believe grief does something to the brain. Certain thoughts which were once inconceivable are now given free rein.

As it turned out, my first true morel site was only a one-year wonder. The following year there was not a single morel to be found in that flower bed in Grünerløkka, although I went back to check two or three times. I just had to accept that the morel carnival was over. Now all my hopes were pinned on the bark-covered bed that I had laid out at the allotment. It usually takes a year or two for true morels to appear, if they appear.

At the allotment I always have my breakfast next to this bark bed, on a little terrace I arranged to have built after Eiolf's death, designed by him for this very purpose. It was one of those building projects that was slightly bigger than I could manage on my own, but I thought it would be nice to come back to the allotment for a new season to find Eiolf's terrace all finished and ready for use. It's not large, but made to measure for our favourite garden furniture. So in the morning I sit on an old, white bench under the cherry tree, eating my porridge and surveying all the glories of the garden. Eiolf was right: it makes the ideal breakfast spot, warmed as it is by the morning sun.

I was sitting there one morning when I did a little double-take — was that something poking through the bark in the bed next to me? I wasn't sure whether it was just some dead rhododendron flowers from our neighbour's plot, so I ran into the cottage to fetch my glasses. My heart skipped a beat when I saw not one, but two true morels growing there.

A week later it was the anniversary of Eiolf's death. When he died, the calendar changed for ever. As well as our wedding anniversary and birthdays there are now other dates to be commemorated. Certain days light up and start flashing long before they arrive.

The anniversary of his death is one of those days. In my head the countdown begins: first weeks, then days, and then, finally, the hours until the second when Eiolf ceased to live. I find it almost impossible to think about anything else, the clock ticks so loudly. Only after that moment can life start rolling again. That year, on the anniversary of his death, I put on my glasses and ran out to the flower bed before putting my porridge on.

Had Eiolf sent me a sign? I came out in goosebumps when I saw a third true morel in the bed.

It was a moment of absolute bliss in which everything else disappeared and there was nothing in the world but me and the morel. This one was smaller than the other two, which had had a whole week in which to grow, but it was slender and tapering and distinct in all its morel-ness. Other people might have thanked God or some other higher power, but I sent a tender salute to the one I know in heaven and thanked him for his caress.

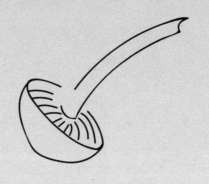

The
mushroom
code

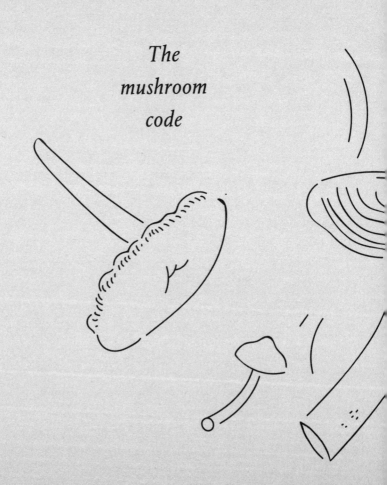

There is really only one rule that everyone should follow:

> **Rule no. 1:** If you are not sure whether a mushroom
> is edible, do not eat it.

The rest of the rules are not so vital. They are simply my own personal recommendations.

> **Rule no. 2:** Take species identification seriously.
> When you are an amateur forager, eager to find
> something edible, there is always a risk of confusing
> a mushroom in the forest with one you have seen
> in a field guide. If you are out with experienced
> mushroomer gatherers it is always wise to ask their
> advice on what to look for in a mushroom you have
> found. The experts sometimes have their own little
> identification tips, ones you won't find in the field
> guides.

Rule no. 3: Always be prepared. I always carry something with which to pick mushrooms and something to put them in. During the season in Norway, from May to December, I never go anywhere without a mushroom knife — there's nothing worse than finding mushrooms and not having any equipment with you. Some people prefer to manage with the minimum of equipment, others arm themselves with a GPS tracker, magnifying glasses, or even a jeweller's loupe, complete with light, to enlarge and inspect interesting details. Find your own style, but always be prepared.

Rule no. 4: Never mix unidentified species with mushrooms you're sure of. It would be a shame to have to throw away all your mushrooms if you find one highly toxic mushroom among all the good edible ones.

Rule no. 5: Do the rough cleaning on the spot. It saves you carrying home a lot of dirt and grit and other debris. I prefer the mushrooms I bring home to be as ready for the frying pan as possible.

Rule no. 6: Take good hand hygiene seriously. Actually it is enough just to wipe your hand on some damp moss. That said, it's important to point out that you can hold a deadly mushroom in your bare hands. They are only lethal when eaten.

Rule no. 7: Join the trips organised by your local society. These will take you to new places and give you the opportunity to get to know fellow enthusiasts.

Rule no. 8: Go foraging with mushroomers who are more knowledgeable and experienced than yourself. It is the best way to learn more. And the more you know, the more pleasure you will get from it.

Rule no. 9: Never stop reading, checking, surfing the Internet, and participating in discussions on social media and elsewhere.

Rule no. 10: Trust your own judgement. Don't simply believe everything you're told — not even by experts — on matters where there is room for personal opinions and interpretations.

Mushroom register

A

Almond Fibrecap, *Inocybe hirtella*

Almond Woodwax, *Hygrophorus agathosmus*

Amethyst Deceiver, *Laccaria amethystina*

Aniseed Funnel Mushroom, *Clitocybe odora*

B

Birch Webcap, *Cortinarius triumphans*

Bitter Beech Bolete, *Boletus calopus*

Blackening Russula, *Russula nigricans*

Bloody Brittlegill, *Russula sanguinea*

Bloody Milk Cap, *Lactarius sanguifluus*

Brain Mushroom, *Gyromitra esculenta*

Burgundydrop Bonnet, *Mycena haematopus*

Button mushrooms, *Agaricus bisporus*

C

Candy Cap, *Lactarius rubidus*

Chanterelle, *Cantharellus cibarius*

Charcoal Burner, *Russula cyanoxantha*

Chepang Slender Caesar, *Amanita chepangiana*

Clouded Agaric, *Clitocybe nebularis*

Coconut Milk Cap, *Lactarius glyciosmus*

Common Ink Cap, *Coprinopsis atramentaria*

common lawn mushroom, *Panaeolina foenisecii*

Common Stinkhorn, *Phallus impudicus* (also known as the Witch's Egg)

Common Yellow Russula, *Russula ochroleuca*

Copper Spike, *Chroogomphus rutilus*

Cortinarius rheubarbarinus

Cortinarius venetus

Crab Brittlegill, *Russula xerampelina*

Cuban Psilocybe, *Psilocybe cubensis*

Cucumber Cap, *Macrocystidia cucumis*

Curry Milk Cap, *Lactarius camphoratus*

D

Dark Honey Fungus, *Armillaria ostoyae*

Deadly Webcap, *Cortinarius rubellus*

Death Cap, *Amanita phalloide*

Destroying Angel, *Amanita virosa*

Devil's Urn, *Urnula craterium*

Dog Stinkhorn, *Mutinus ravenelii*

F

false chanterelle, *Hygrophoropsis aurantiaca*

Fenugreek Milk Cap, *Lactarius helvus*

Fly Agaric, *Amanita muscaria*

Freckled Dapperling, *Echinoderma asperum*

Funeral Bell, *Galerina marginata*

Funnel chanterelle, *Craterellus tubaeformis*

G

Gassy Webcap, *Cortinarius traganus*

Giant Knight, *Tricholoma colossus*

Giant Puffball, *Calvatia gigantea*

Goat Moth Wax Cap, *Hygrophorus cossus*

Goatcheese Webcap, *Cortinarius camphoratus*

Grey Veiled Amanita, *Amanita porphyria*

Gypsy Mushroom, *Cortinarius caperatus*

H

Hawaiian Blue Meanie, *Panaeolus cyanescens*

Hedgehog Mushroom, *Hydnum repandum*

Honey Fungus, *Armillaria mellea*

Horn of Plenty, *Craterellus cornucopioides*

Horse Mushroom, *Agaricus arvensis*

Hydnellum suaveolens

Hygrocybe foetens

J

Jack o' Lantern, *Omphalotus olearius*

Jersey Cow Mushroom, *Suillus bovinus*

L

Liberty Cap, *Psilocybe semilanceata* (also known as magic mushrooms)

Lingzhi Mushroom, *Ganoderma lucidum*

Lurid Bolete, *Suillellus luridus*

Luxuriant Ringstalk, *Stropharia hornemannii*

M

Matsutake, *Tricholoma matsutake* (also known as the Pine Mushroom)

Meadow Mushroom, *Agaricus campestris*

Miller Mushroom, *Clitopilus prunulus*

O

Orange Birch Bolete, *Leccinum versipelle*

Orange Milk Cap, *Lactarius deterrimus*

Orange Peel Fungus, *Aleuria aurantia*

Overflowing Slimy Stem, *Limacella illinita*

Oyster mushroom, *Pleurotus ostreatus*

P

Paddy Straw Mushroom, *Volvariella volvacea*

Parasol Mushroom, *Macrolepiota procera*

Pelargonium Webcap, *Cortinarius paleaceus*

Penny Bun, *Boletus edulis* (also known as King Bolete, porcini, cep)

Peppery Bolete, *Chalciporus piperatus*

Pink Bonnet, *Mycena rosella*

Poison Pie, *Hebeloma crustuliniforme*

Poor Man's Pepper, *Lepidium virginicum*

Powdery Brittlegill, *Russula parazurea*

Prince mushroom, *Agaricus augustus*

Q

Quilted Green Russula, *Russula virescens*

R

Red-Banded Webcap, *Cortinarius armillatus*

Ringless Honey Mushroom, *Armillaria tabescens*

Rooting Poison Pie, *Hebeloma radicosum*

Rosy Spike-Cap, *Gomphidius roseus*

Russula odorata

S

Saffrondrop Bonnet, *Mycena crocata*

Saffron Milk Cap, *Lactarius deliciosus*

Salty Mushroom, *Agaricus bernardii*

Scaly Wood Mushroom, *Agaricus langei*

Scarlet Bonnet, *Mycena adonis*

Scotch Bonnet, *Marasmius oreades*

Shaggy Ink Cap, *Coprinus comatus*

Sheathed Woodtuft, *Pholiota mutabilis*

Sheep Polypore, *Albatrellus ovinus*

shiitake mushroom, *Lentinus edodes*

Shingled Hedgehog, *Sarcodon imbricatus*

Spring Orange Peel Fungus, *Caloscypha fulgens*

St George's mushroom, *Calocybe gambosa*

Stinking Dapperling, *Lepiota cristata*

Stinking Russula, *Russula foetens*

summer cep, *Boletus reticulatus*

Sweet Poison Pie, *Hebeloma sacchariolens*

T

Tawny Milk Cap, *Lactarius volemus*
Tawny Webcap, *Cortinarius callisteus*
Termitomyces titanicus
Tiny Earthstar, *Geastrum minimum*
Tolypocladium inflatum
true morel, *Morchella conica*

V

Velvet Bolete, *Suillus variegatus*
Velvet Brittlegill, *Russula violeipes*

W

Waxy Laccaria, *Laccaria laccata*
White Fibrecap, *Inocybe geophylla*
White King Bolete, *Boletus barrowsii*
White Webcap, *Leucocortinarius bulbiger*
Winter Mushroom, *Flammulina velutipes*

Witches' Cauldron, *Sarcosoma globosum*
Witch's Egg, *Phallus impudicus*
Wood Blewit, *Lepista nuda*
Wood Mushroom, *Agaricus sylvicola*
Wood Pinkgill, *Entoloma rhodopolium*

Y

Yellow Foot Mushroom, *Craterellus lutescens*
Yellow Knight, *Tricholoma equestre* (also known as the Man on Horseback)
Yellow-staining Mushroom, *Agaricus xanthodermus*
Yellow Swamp Russula, *Russula claroflava*

Bibliography

Borgarino, Didier. (2011). *Champignons de Provence.* France: Edisud.

de Caprona, Yann. (2013). *Norsk etymologisk ordbok.* Oslo: Kagge Forlag.

Cook, Langdon. (2013). *The Mushroom Hunters: on the trail of an underground America.* New York: Ballantine Books.

Gennep, Arnold van. (2010). *The rites of passage.* Translated by Monika B. Vizedom & Gabrielle L. Caffee. London: Routledge.

Gulden, Gro. (2013). «De ekte morklene», i *Sopp og nyttevekster*, årgang 9, nr. 2/2013 (s. 28–33).

Høiland, Klaus and Ryvarden, Leif. (2014). *Er det liv, er det sopp!* Oslo: Dreyer.

Lincoff, Gary. (2010). *The National Audubon Society Field Guide to North American Mushrooms.* New York: Knopf.

Mauss, Marcel. (1969). *The Gift: forms and functions of exchange in archaic societies.* Translated by Ian Cunnison. London: Cohen & West.

Sopp, Olav J. (1883). *Spiselig Sop: Dens indsamling, opbevaring og tilberedning.* Kristiania: Cammermeyer.

Wasson, R. Gordon. (1980). *The Wondrous Mushroom: mycolatry in Mesoamerica.* New York: McGraw-Hill.

Weber, Nancy. S. (1988). *A Morel Hunter's Companion: a guide to the true and false morels of Michigan.* Michigan: Two Peninsula Press.

Wright, John. (2007). *Mushrooms: the River Cottage handbook.* London: Bloomsbury Publishing.

Unprinted sources

Replies to questionnaire from the Norwegian Ethnological Research (NEG) at the Norwegian Folk Museum.

List of psilocybin trip levels, quoted from www.shroomery.org

Notes

1. Stamets, Paul. (2008) '6 Ways Mushrooms Can Save the World', TED Talk, https://www.ted.com/talks/paul_stamets_on_6_ways_mushrooms_can_save_the_world
2. NEG 175 *Sopp og Bær*: No. 33108
3. NEG 175 *Sopp og Bær*: No. 32775
4. NEG 175 *Sopp og bær*: No. 32938
5. NEG 175 *Sopp og bær*: No. 32854
6. NEG 175 *Sopp og bær*: No. 32854

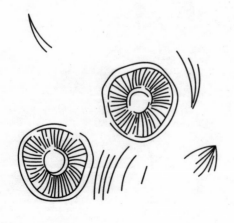